Breaking White

An Introduction to Breaking Bad

By Pearson Moore

Books by Pearson Moore:

LOST Humanity
The Mythology and Themes of LOST

LOST Humanity University Edition

LOST Identity: The Characters of LOST

LOST Thought: Leading Thinkers Discuss LOST

LOST Thought University Edition

Cartier's Ring: A Novel of Canada

Deneb (science fiction novel, coming in 2013)

Game of Thrones Season One Essays

Game of Thrones Season One Essays, Illustrated Edition

Game of Thrones Season Two Essays, Illustrated Edition

Breaking White

An Introduction to Breaking Bad

Covering the first season of Breaking Bad

By Pearson Moore

Featuring illustrations by
Martin Woutisseth
and
Michael Rainey

Breaking White
An Introduction to Breaking Bad

Cover concept and design by Michael Rainey

Printed by Inukshuk Press

ISBN: 978-0-61-571985-6

To my high school chemistry teacher,

Frederick P. Buechler

Science Department Chairman
John Marshall Senior High School
Rochester, Minnesota

Table of the Elements

1 H 1.01																	2 He 4.00
3 Li 6.94	4 Be 9.01											5 B 10.81	6 C 12.01	7 N 14.01	8 O 16.00	9 F 19.00	10 Ne 20.18
11 Na 22.99	12 Mg 24.31											13 Al 26.58	14 Si 28.09	15 P 30.97	16 S 32.07	17 Cl 35.45	18 Ar 39.95
19 K 39.10	20 Ca 40.08											31 Ga 69.72	32 Ge 72.61	33 As 74.92	34 Se 78.96	35 Br 79.50	36 Kr 83.80
37 Rb 85.47	38 Sr 87.62											49 In 114.82	50 Sn 118.71	51 Sb 121.76	52 Te 127.60	53 I 126.90	54 Xe 131.29

Table of Contents

Introduction to Breaking White

Breaking Bad Splash
Copyright 2012 Martin Woutisseth
Used with permission

"Maybe the universe is trying to tell me something."

We will hear these words only a few times in the course of Breaking Bad. They will be uttered at odd moments, not highlighted or showcased in any way, given breath by dejected characters, entering our awareness not so much through our senses as through the central core of our consciousness.

Breaking Bad is morality play on a scale rarely attempted. It does not paint a fictional environment we can enter and exit at our fancy, but rather tells us of our own world. It paints reality not as an optional element of life that can be taken or abandoned at will, but the primary feature of our relation to each other and to this "universe" that is trying to tell us something.

The primal sense that the universe has structure and priority and value will come to the fore at unpredictable moments during the show. For me, one of those eerie moments was at the table in Jesse Pinkman's kitchen, when Walter White focused all of his intellect and emotion on the broken shards of a yellow ceramic plate. A utensil which no longer served its purpose, discarded as worthless trash, suddenly carried such value as to become the most meaningful item in Walter's world. He would see in the jagged, ill-fitting pieces a set of instructions calling upon him to make a crucial decision about the priorities he would apply to his life.

Many such "aha" moments occur in the series. Some will experience the smoke from Hank Schrader's Cuban cigar as an epiphany. Others will see in Gustavo Fring's pressed yellow button-down service shirt an electrifying statement of the unyielding tension holding the characters in their places, forcing them into confrontation, demanding an irrevocable exercise of volition. We sense in these scenes a plan, an objective—some force of nature that compels us to take a stand based on precepts we accept.

Some of us will construct from the yellow shards of broken ceramic a set of precepts incongruent with the unyielding tension and final destiny of the universe. Walter White, we will come to realize, is one of those whose arrangement of fragmented pieces will bring him into fundamental opposition with that destiny. But he is not the only one who will manufacture untenable hierarchies of misplaced value. During the course of Breaking Bad many characters—even some we initially believe to have a sound philosophy of life—will render decisions unacceptable to society, to the laws of the State of New Mexico, or to their relationships with family and friends.

Why "Breaking White"?

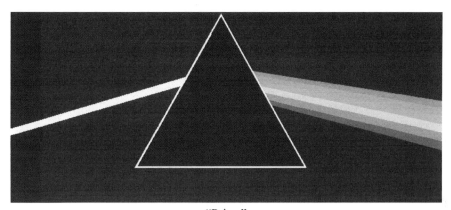

"Prism"
Pearson Moore 2012

To "Break Bad" means "to go wild, get crazy, let loose, forget all your cares ... have a great time, break out of your mold." It can also mean "To challenge convention, defy authority ... to skirt the edge of the law." (Urban Dictionary, 2006-2011). When I say "Breaking White," though, I am using the word "breaking" in quite a different sense, more along the lines of an intense, open-ended discussion. To "break a story," for instance, means to brainstorm the plot and structure of a novel, play, or movie. The phrase is used by writers to describe the process of taking a basic concept or bare-bones plot and turning it into an interesting, dramatic, conflict-drenched story.

"Breaking White" refers to an intense process through which we examine, discuss, and debate the symbolic, dramatic, and plot-related significance of White—both the symbol White and the character Walter White. We engage in this close discussion neither as writers nor as viewers. I consider that an unengaged observer or viewer lacks the emotional connection and intellectual immersion necessary to understand Breaking Bad at multiple levels. Only those who go to the next level, who become *viewer-participants*, who become part of the story, are able to appreciate Breaking Bad to the fullest extent possible.

This book is called *Breaking White* because we will focus our discussion of the first season of Breaking Bad on the character of Walter White, the symbolic significance of his name, and the beginnings of his transition to the drug lord, Heisenberg. *Breaking Blue*, on the other hand, covers the entire five seasons of Breaking Bad and delves into the deeper significance of the themes, thesis, and colors of Breaking Bad. I consider that Blue is the visual statement of Breaking Bad's thesis; "Breaking Blue," then, refers to an attempt to dig into and understand the core of Breaking Bad philosophy, themes, and symbols.

Skewed, Twisted, and Fried

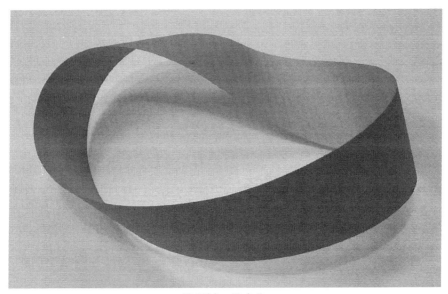

"Möbius Strip"
Photograph copyright 2005 David Benbennick, CC-SA 3.0

Breaking Bad appeals at many levels. The show not only incorporates heavy symbolism at every turn, but it turns symbols upside down and inside out, it approaches metaphor within metaphor.

Good guys do bad things that result in unexpected boons to peripheral players. Bad guys sometimes do good things for entirely unselfish reasons. Legality, morality, motivation and virtue are juxtaposed and mixed and melded into situations that force us to re-examine our own values, to re-think our priorities.

Consider, for example, this truth: Everyone reading these words is a criminal. Yes, *you*, not the person sitting next to you. You are a criminal who has made choices that endanger women and men. You have put children at risk. You regularly court the possibility of severe fines and penalties, and jail time. If you are lucky your criminality will not result in suffering or death. But these destructive actions do eventually result in misery and horrible, grisly deaths. Yet you persist in your criminal behavior. You justify it. You embrace it.

Breaking Bad never addresses the fact that 99% of drivers in the United States exceed the speed limit by an average of seven miles per hour, as I did in the paragraph above. But it confronts other equally sobering truths about the way we choose to live our lives, and does so in an unapologetic, in-your-face manner that ought to repulse, but only attracts.

Breaking Bad is enormously entertaining, masterfully conceived and executed serialized storytelling of the highest order. I am not alone in considering it the best series currently on television, but I have special reasons for considering it so.

For one thing, I am a chemist. I've taught high school chemistry. Not only that, but my deepest area of expertise is in crystallization, and my broadest region of expertise includes the efficient extraction and purification of high-value chemicals from biological sources. I have been doing this type of work since the mid-1970s. If I were interested in manufacturing methamphetamine, I have the expertise to create a product every bit as pure as Walter White's. If I wished, I could isolate deadly ricin or any other highly toxic material, and I could quickly and easily create delivery systems for efficient ingestion. I know how to poison people and how to turn a dead body into unrecognizable glop. I am about the same age as Walter White, with similar background and credentials.

I appreciate Breaking Bad, then, as a technical "insider," and this close knowledge of the scientific side of the show has resulted mostly in my admiration. Breaking Bad takes no shortcuts, makes no excuses, and adheres in most ways to an intellectually authentic vision of science as it is actually done. That is not to say that everything portrayed on the show is scientifically or technically correct. In particular, as you might have guessed, you should definitely not try to cook methamphetamine according to the Breaking Bad formula. You'll only create a mess.

My fluency in the technical aspects of the production only contributes to my awareness and enjoyment of the artistic aspects of the show. Chemistry is developed into the primary metaphor for Walter White's descent into moral depravity, but chemistry and science themselves are never sullied. Although the series is not yet complete as I write these words, I have several independent bases for believing that the purity of science, the fact that we "must respect the chemistry," is integral to the point Vince Gilligan wishes to make about Walter White, and therefore about our world.

Consequences, Change, Conflict

What is the nature of the Breaking Bad universe? Does consequence follow action inevitably in always-predictable fashion? Does an outcome depend on the inputs to the situation, with the calculus of retribution tied to so many variables that we cannot foresee the effect our actions will have in the world? Or is the world constructed in some other way, with constraints of cause and effect we have not imagined in our daily decisions and debates?

We will experience over five seasons innumerable instances of consequences. We will spy on characters as they devise simple plans, well engineered to account for every contingency, thought out to the smallest detail and possibility, that will nevertheless fail through unintended, under-appreciated, or unconsidered complications.

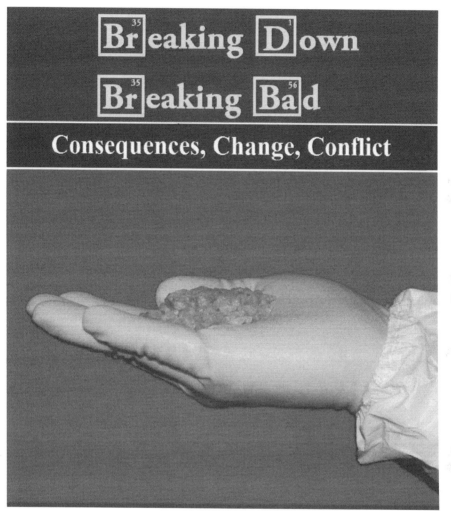

"Crystal Blue Perfusion"
Photograph Copyright 2012 Pearson Moore
Created for *Breaking Blue: The Themes, Thesis and Colors of Breaking Bad*

"If there's a larger lesson to 'Breaking Bad,' it's that actions have consequences." (Vince Gilligan, New York Times interview, 10 July 2011) Often the outcome is unforeseen, despite the best-laid plans, and the result is black comedy of the most stinging and delicious and hilarious nature. Occasionally a well-considered action results in intentional or unpredicted anguish, misery, and death. Judgment will, at times, literally rain down from the heavens. "I feel some sort of need for biblical atonement, or justice, or something," Gilligan said. "I like to believe there is some comeuppance, that karma kicks in at some point, even if it takes years or decades to happen." (Vince Gilligan, New York Times interview, 10 July 2011)

The manner in which characters resolve to address consequence inevitably leads to both success and failure. As characters learn from mistakes and triumphs, they re-evaluate priorities and values, they adapt to future challenges. They change. The adaptations are conscious, intentional, and tuned closely to the events surrounding the players. Much of the mayhem, destruction, and horror we experience will have been meticulously planned and executed by decision makers aware of the upheavals their actions will wreak in others' lives. "For the first time in a long, long while I am not sleepwalking through life, I am awake." (www.waltswisdom.com, Entry of October 19, downloaded 20 October 2012)

Not every change will be for the worse. In fact, many viewer-participants will be able to make a case that Walter White's transition to Heisenberg includes the acquisition of positive, life-affirming attributes. I agree with this assessment. I believe we short-change ourselves and derive less benefit from the series if we do not consider the many ways in which all of the characters adapt to the subtle and severe changes in their environment. In particular, several of the characters we initially consider to form the bedrock of sensible, sober, and moral living will at some point begin to exhibit behaviors that could only be considered immoral or sociopathic.

We need not authorize moral *carte blanche*, for any character. "Journalists … will say to me, 'How are we supposed to like [Walter]?' And I say, 'Are you supposed to? Where's the rule that says you're supposed to follow some edict?' All the rules are broken, you can go anywhere." (Bryan Cranston, interview on hypable.com, 18 October 2012) We don't have to dance around our feelings about characters, equip them with excuses or alibis, or try to rationalize any of their actions. "Vince Gilligan … believes his main character, … meth dealer Walter White, should go straight to hell." (Martin Miller, Los Angeles Times, 1 September 2012) Each of us has license, then, to think anything our consciences tell us we should feel about each character.

The extreme circumstances imposed by radical change and pursuit of extraordinary personal gain will bring about unusual, morally challenging events and create strange bedfellows. This is demonstrated in many of the close relationships between main characters, the most obvious being Walter White's complicated ties to his DEA brother-in-law, Hank Schrader. But irony and topsy-turvy ethics will play out in almost every relationship and are intentionally built into the conflict-ridden fabric of the show.

In particular, Breaking Bad achieves something rarely portrayed on television or in cinema: credible family relationships. For reasons I will discuss later in this book, families are usually the first aspect of reality excised from any fictional characterization of human life. Breaking Bad, though, relishes the situational, emotional, psychological, and storytelling complexity imposed by the realistic demands of family interaction. As a writer and storyteller myself, I appreciate this insistence on the unabashed confrontation of messy, real-life scenarios. Neither hero nor villain operates in a vacuum in Breaking Bad. Family is not only important, but it is the center of every major event of the series. "La familia es todo," as one character will say. This kind of storytelling is rare, not because it is in any way irrelevant, but because it requires the most expert implementation of the storytelling arts. Quite simply, most authors are not up to the mind-numbing rigors of realistic storytelling focusing on multiple players with conflicting and ongoing agendas. In Breaking Bad we are witnesses and privileged participants in the rarest of cinematic creations.

How To Use This Book

The Thinker
Auguste Rodin, circa 1902
Photograph by Hans Anderson, placed in PD 2005

This book is probably different from other television guidebooks you have read. Those who have read *LOST Humanity* have a good idea of what to expect. For instance, I don't consider it my job to *explain* anything. I am not an expert in human behavior. I have no experience in theater, I hold no degrees in film theory or literary analysis. I wouldn't know neoformalism from postmodern constructivism. The volume you see before you is definitely not an academic treatise, and I hold no pretensions of rising to any level of intellectual rigor or consistency.

My objective in this book is to pose questions and to stimulate thought. I will discuss ideas I believe relevant to the *enjoyment* of Breaking Bad. There are no truths in these pages. I do not possess insider knowledge regarding Vince Gilligan's intentions, Aaron Paul's artistic interpretations, or scholarly positions on Breaking Bad concepts or symbols.

I hope you will consider every statement in this book as a starting point for your own contemplation of the television series. You are not obliged to believe as I do. You are not required to construct arguments as I have, or to prioritize ideas and enumerate symbolic interactions as I do. In fact, I hope many of you disagree. Without diversity of opinion and insight there is no basis for discussion. Art is meant to be discussed, weighed, considered, and re-evaluated.

1 H 1.01							2 He 4.00
3 Li 6.94	4 Be 9.01	5 B 10.81	6 C 12.01	7 N 14.01	8 O 16.00	9 F 19.00	10 Ne 20.18
11 Na 22.99	12 Mg 24.31	13 Al 26.58	14 Si 28.09	15 P 30.97	16 S 32.07	17 Cl 35.45	18 Ar 39.95
19 K 39.10	20 Ca 40.08	31 Ga 69.72	32 Ge 72.61	33 As 74.92	34 Se 78.96	35 Br 79.50	36 Kr 83.80
37 Rb 85.47	38 Sr 87.62	49 In 114.82	50 Sn 118.71	51 Sb 121.76	52 Te 127.60	53 I 126.90	54 Xe 131.29

Periodic Table of the Elements for *Breaking Blue*
Excluding the Transition Elements

Breaking White is the first part of *Breaking Blue*. You will gain the most from the discussion in *Breaking White* if you have seen or are beginning to watch the first season of Breaking Bad. The first prologue ("Walter") discusses mostly the first episode, but the second prologue ("White") refers to important scenes as late as Episode 1.05. Although I may mention later episodes of Breaking Bad, you will not need to have seen any episode after 1.07 ("A No-Rough-Stuff Type Deal") in order to follow my discussion.

Both *Breaking White* and *Breaking Blue* are arranged according to the elements of the periodic table. *Breaking White* occupies the first period of the periodic table, which spans only two elements: Hydrogen and Helium. The second period, included only in *Breaking Blue*, begins with Lithium (Li) and continues to Neon (Ne).

Scientists and those readers familiar with the periodic table of the elements will observe that the table above excludes the transition elements. This is because in the *Breaking Blue* scheme each period of the periodic table corresponds to one season of Breaking Bad. Since each season (except the first) will have no more than five to eight chapters, I won't need the transition elements.

The table format may seem a bit odd, but there is precedent. Dmitri Mendeleev's second periodic table (1871) used a similar format.

Careful readers will note that the first chapter after the second prologue is Chapter H (for hydrogen, the first element), but this entry is not followed by Chapter He, which is the next element in the period table. Instead, Chapter H is followed by Chapter D.

Mendeleev's Periodic Table of 1871

	I	II	III	IV RH$_4$	V RH$_3$	VI RH$_2$	VII RH	VIII
	--- R$_2$0	--- RO	--- R$_2$O$_3$	RO$_2$	R$_2$O$_.$	RO$_3$	R$_2$O$_.$	--- RO$_4$
1	H 1							
2	Li 7	Be 9.4	B 11	C 12	N 14	O 16	F 19	
3	Na 23	Mg 24	Al 27.3	Si 28	P 31	S 32	Cl 35.5	
4	K 39	Ca 40	? 44	Ti 48	V 51	Cr 52	Mn 55	Fe, Co, Ni,Cu 56, 59, 59, 63
5	Cu 63	Zn 65	? 68	? 72	As 75	Se 78	Br 80	
6	Rb 85	Sr 87	? Yt 88	Zr 90	Nb 94	Mo 96	? 100	Ru, Rh. Pd, Ag 104, 104, 106, 108
7	Ag 108	Cd 112	In 113	Sn 118	Sb 122	Te 125	I 127	
8	Cs 133	Ba 137	? Di 138	? Ce 140	?	?	?	?, ?, ?, ?
9	?	?	?	?	?	?	?	
10	?	?	? Er 178	?? La 180	Ta 182	W 184	?	Os, Ir, Pt, Au 195, 197, 198, 199
11	Au 199	Hg 200	Tl 204	Pb 207	Bi 208	?	?	
12	?	?	?	Th 231	?	U 240	?	

Mendeleev's 2nd Periodic Table, 1871

There is no Element D in any periodic table of the elements, but I have used sound scientific reasoning to include this chapter immediately following Chapter H. The rationale takes into account concepts critical to our discussion of Breaking Bad. To understand my thinking you will need to read the book. I invite you now to begin the adventure of *Breaking White*.

PM
October 15, 2012

Walter White by Michael Rainey
used with permission

Prologue I

Mr. Chips becomes Scarface.

In almost every interview he has granted, this is the phrase Vince Gilligan has employed to describe the character arc, and the primary focus, of Breaking Bad. An ordinary fellow, a doting father and beloved high school teacher, is transformed before our eyes into the most despicable and vicious of criminals, a modern-day embodiment of evil.

If these four words accurately described the totality of Breaking Bad we would have no reason to marvel at the thoughts and emotions effervescing in our minds. There are aspects of Breaking Bad that go beyond the raw dramatic power of the scenes, the tour-de-force acting by talented actors, and the extraordinary voyage into the heart of the despicable and the damned. The most important elements of Breaking Bad are those that evade our immediate perception, that lurk in the background of our conscious selves, that burst forth not as logical assessments of character or plot, but as emotional revelations of primal identity.

At some point in the series we are repulsed by Walter White. We hold out hope for his redemption, for an episode or a season or three seasons. But at some point, the hope and charity and good will in our hearts are displaced by pragmatism—or heartfelt demands for tempered justice or untempered retribution. Some composers and artists beg that we withhold judgment. There are no such entreaties from the creators of Breaking Bad. Vince Gilligan "believes his main character, high school chemistry teacher turned meth dealer Walter White, should go straight to hell." (Martin Miller, Los Angeles Times, 1 Sep 2012) We are given *carte blanche* to act as judge and jury in approving or condemning the actions and essential core of the characters in Breaking Bad.

But if this were our only means of interacting with the characters, nothing would distinguish Walter White and Tuco Salamanca and Gustavo Fring from the cardboard cut-out characters in the boring-as-hell procedural dramas that are a blight on 21st century television. Breaking Bad is not a 60-episode-long whodunit. It is not even a whydunit. Discerning the motivations of Walter White is integral to the enjoyment of the show, but personal rationale is not the central question of the series.

The primal center of Breaking Bad is not Walter White, but our personal reaction to him. At some point in the series, all of us will become united in our disgust and absolute contempt for Walter White. But the most interesting aspect of the drama is that we will arrive at this point in different ways, with unique sets of unconscious circumstances and considerations weighing on our conscious decision to consign him to the dark folds of our scorn and disdain.

The brilliance of Vince Gilligan's creation, though, is not that it arouses our righteous indignation, or that it stirs in us a sense of justice or a desire to see karma run its course. If this were the only objective, we could satisfy the urge with any courtroom drama or testosterone-filled action-adventure movie of the 1980s.

Every one of us will paint a different portrait of Walter White. The colors and lines and features we use to paint this portrait depend not so much on the facets of the character on the screen, and not to any particular isolated notion we have regarding a facet of his personality. More than anything, our personal and widely varying concepts of good and evil, humanity and integrity, and identity as responsible human beings will have direct bearing on our assessment of Walter. But these aspects of thought and disposition are not evoked in series or in a vacuum. Rather, Breaking Bad forces simultaneous consideration of several distinct but inter-connected thoughts and emotions. The grandeur of Breaking Bad is found in the ***multiplicity*** of ways it forces personal connection with us, the audience-participants.

That Breaking Bad creates multi-dimensional characters and a fascinating fictional world places it among the better dramas of 21st century television. That the series accomplishes all this and also drives our emotions and compels our unreserved intellectual and personal participation places the show at the pinnacle of artistic creation. Some of the most discerning and hard-to-please television and pop culture critics consider Breaking Bad the most meaningful series ever to have appeared on television. It achieves this distinction because it appeals to us in rare and profound ways.

The focal point of our enchantment is the character we will love to hate: Walter Hartwell White. If we are to arrive at a deeper appreciation of our feelings and thoughts about this man, we will have to devote some time to understanding his origins, his motivations, and the personal and social constructions that define him as a unique individual. I believe that in order to do this properly we are going to have to move beyond the four-word description of his character arc. In fact, I believe we are going to have to discard the notion that a complete or even adequate portrait of Walter White begins with a consideration of Mr. Chips. Two other characters from 1930s literature are essential to our understanding of Walter White, and if we truly wish to unveil the man's complexity, I believe we need to reach back all the way to mid-19th century New York City, to a chill night in October, 1858, when a frail, sickly child was delivered into the world. But let us begin with a closer look at Walter White.

Walter Hartwell White

I am not going to catalog here every one of the characteristics of Walter White. My objective in this first of two prologue essays is to identify what we might call the "origins" of Walter White—those aspects of his character that informed his lifestyle and life choices prior to his decision to break bad. Facets of his identity that move beyond his character arc and impinge on plot trajectory, such as Walter's vocation of chemistry teacher and the deeper meaning of his surname, are important enough that they will receive their own essays and will not be developed here. In the case of Walter's last name, for instance, the word 'White' is not merely a surname, but also a color that in itself is an important motif in the story.

Man Suppressed

The script for the second scene of the pilot episode specified that Walter was dressed in tans and browns—colors intentionally chosen for their blandness, such that he would blend into the browns, pastel greens, and beiges of the dining room and kitchen. Bryan Cranston grew a moustache and thinned it out so it looked like a "dead caterpillar." Cranston's intention was to make Walter White appear as "impotent" as possible.

House Mouse
National Institutes of Health, 2004, PD

Walter White is man emasculated. He is less than he should be, less than he could be, held captive by and subordinate to forces we cannot know with certainty. Rather than "wearing the pants" and leading the family as father, he has become the subordinate parent, neither the head of the family nor even an equal partner to his hard-charging wife, Skyler. The importance of this point to the story is impressed on us in the second scene after the opening flash-forward in the pilot episode.

Skyler: [Placing in front of Walter a plate of eggs and artificial bacon] Happy birthday!
Walter: [Disappointed or surprised] Look at that.
Skyler: *That* is veggie bacon, believe it or not. Zero cholesterol and you won't even taste the difference. What time do you think you'll be home?
Walter: Same time.
Skyler: I don't want 'em dicking you around tonight. You get paid 'til five, you work 'til five, no later.

In the space of just 32 seconds we learn from this dialog one of the most important truths about Walter White: he is ruled by his wife. She decides what he will have for breakfast, and she even decides whether he will enjoy it or not. She decides how long he will work and precisely when he will return home. If there is a problem at work, she, not Walter, lays down the law.

More importantly, though, we learn that Skyler is not the only person pushing Walter around. We understand from the context of Skyler's words that Walter's employers at the car wash have been habitually "dicking him around," a phrase rich with meaning, especially in the stifling atmosphere of the Whites' breakfast table on the morning of Walter's 50th birthday.

As important as these first few seconds are to our assessment of Walter, the events of the next minute are even more important, for it is in this crucial moment that we learn Walter could choose to behave in a very different way.

Skyler: [To Junior] You're late … again.
Junior: There was no hot water, *again*.
Skyler: I have an easy fix for that: You wake up early and then you get to be the first person in the shower.
Junior: I have an idea: Buy a new hot water heater. How's that idea, for the millionth, millionth time.

Junior is behaving as a normal, slightly rebellious teenager, but more important to our analysis of Walter White, he is demonstrating the possibility of standing up to Skyler and her dictates. This brief interaction demonstrates that Walter does not have to acquiesce. He could assert himself and his needs and desires if he wished. For some reason or set of reasons, though, he has chosen to cave.

Junior: [Examining the artificial bacon] What *the hell* is this?
Skyler: [Expressing parental disapproval] Hey!
Walter: Veggie bacon. We're watching our cholesterol … I guess.
Junior: Not me. I want real bacon, not this fake crap.
Skyler: Too bad. Eat it.
Junior: Phew. This smells like Band-Aids.
Skyler: Eat. It.
Junior: [Makes a face at Skyler]
Skyler: [Makes a face back]
Junior: [Looks away and sighs, disgusted with his mother but finally accepting her authority]

Bacon was not an arbitrary choice in this scene. Bacon carries symbolic significance with devastating importance to Walter's standing as father, husband, and provider.

First of all, notice again that Junior is pushing back against Skyler's rules. In fact, he asserts that his desire is more important than her fiat: "Not me. I want real bacon, not this fake crap." The contrast with Walter's nearly unspoken acquiescence to the presence of artificial food on his plate is striking. But because the food under discussion is bacon, Junior is symbolically doing much more than underscoring Walter's status as emasculated lackey to his wife.

A provider is one who "brings home the bacon." We are to understand that in his rejection of "fake crap" Junior is not speaking only for himself, but for masculine propriety in general. He was forcefully directing our attention to the incongruity—to the subversion of masculine prerogative—exemplified by a **woman's** decision to replace real bacon (symbolically, the value that a man brings to his family) with artificial bacon. Symbolically, Skyler was asserting that Walter was not the provider for their family.

A real man works hard, and by the sweat of his brow, brings home the bacon. He brings home not only the resources that provide the necessities of life, but the spice of life, the little extra things that make family life pleasurable. One of those extras is bacon.

Hogs and Pigs Inventory 2002

1 Dot = 15,000 hogs and pigs.
U. S. total is 64,405,103 hogs and pigs.

Source: U.S. Department of Agriculture, Economic Research Service, based on data from National Agricultural Statistics Service.

Vince Gilligan grew up in Richmond, Virginia. While hogs are not a major livestock item on Virginia farms, they are plentiful just across the border in North Carolina. In fact, North Carolina is the second largest producer of hogs after Iowa, and the residents of Virginia are major consumers of North Carolina pork. I am not privy to Vince Gilligan's home life as a child, but I know that he and his closest friends would have been quite familiar with pork as an essential component of Virginia culture. As Azrael, a Jewish resident of the Southern United States noted, "Sorry guys, as much as I love ya, I'm going to have to be a lapsed Jew. A breakfast without bacon is like a day without air down here in Dixie." (Contributor Azrael, found at http://littlegreenfootballs.com/article/6425_Love_Letter_from_Lon don/comments/, April 30, 2003) Or as Glenn from Dallas noted, "A breakfast without bacon is like kissing your sister: It's just not right." (Glenn/Dallas, http://dallasdigestforum.com/, 26 June 2010.)

I point out these cultural facts about bacon because while I don't know the cultural status of bacon in Albuquerque, I am somewhat conversant with Southern tradition, and I know the culture of Dixie had significant bearing on Vince Gilligan's early life. I don't know that Gilligan consciously chose bacon as the focal point of the first two minutes of Breaking Bad, but the symbolic import of this common breakfast food seems not only obvious, but a natural extrapolation from Gilligan's personal experience.

The fact that Skyler could trump a man's real bacon and substitute for it a woman's artificial bacon means that Walter was not truly a provider. He was not truly a man. He was not truly a father. When Junior used words considered inappropriate, it was Skyler, not Walter, who called him on his unseemly language. As Bogdan Wolynetz, Walter's boss, would later say, it is Skyler, not Walter, who "wears the pants" in the White family.

Just as the choice of bacon as focal point in the breakfast scene was not accidental or arbitrary, so too the placement of "dicking around" in Skyler's ultimatum was not the result of unexamined fiat. "Dicking around" in the immediate context of Skyler's instructions meant to mistreat, to play with someone, to force someone to do things they do not wish to do. However, in the greater context of the breakfast scene, we are not out of line if we connect the verb 'to dick' to the noun 'dick,' which is the most common slang term for penis. Approached from this point of view, we could understand that when Skyler said Walter should not allow his employers to continue "dicking [him] around" she meant Walter (who is not a real man because he does not bring home the bacon) should not allow himself to be pushed around by real men (who aggressively dicked him around). Or to the crux of the harsh symbolic significance of Skyler's words, Walter, who symbolically lacks a dick should not allow himself to be pushed around by real men who have dicks.

It's a Cruel World After All

We are given a few well-placed indications that something more than Walter's decision to live in impotence may be at play in this drama. At 18:42 in the pilot episode Walter acknowledges the condition that is causing his coughing fits and physical weakness: Inoperable Stage 3A lung cancer. "Best case scenario, with chemo, I'll live maybe another couple of years." Immediately following the scene in the doctor's office Skyler confronts him with another encroachment of the cruel world into their middle class reality.

Skyler: Did you use the Mastercard last month?   Ah, $15.88 at Staples?
Walter: Um … oh, we needed printer paper.
Skyler: Walt, the Mastercard's the one we *don't* use.
Walter: Okay.
Skyler: So, how was your day?
Walter: [Having just received news he will soon die] Oh, well, you know … I don't know … it was … fine. [smiles]

Walter may be the victim of forces over which he has no control. Even though he is not a smoker, and it is unlikely that exposure to chemicals impinged on his health, nevertheless he has contracted a rare, aggressive case of nonsmoker lung cancer. In addition, even though Walter does not seem to have spent extravagantly (his choice of a Pontiac Aztek is probably meant not only as a sign of poor taste, but also as an indication of obsessive frugality), he owns at least one credit card that is causing some degree of financial distress for the family.

I don't want to downplay the importance of cruel fate or undeserved destiny to the greater story of Breaking Bad, but I wish to defer a discussion of social forces and "acts of God" to later chapters in this book. Fate has not been kind to Walter White, but rather than attempting an analysis of forces beyond human control, I want to concentrate on Walter's reaction to his diagnosis and the place he occupies in the world.

The Rape of Kitty Dukakis

Walter's reaction to his diagnosis is not only unusual, it is unsettling. He has just been told that he has inoperable cancer. If he agrees to the most aggressive treatment regime possible he might live another two years. Even if he does live, though, he will be barely conscious for most of that time. Through unending cycles of chemotherapy, radiation, nausea, weakness, vomiting, hair loss, susceptibility to sudden infection, he will hardly be living a life anyone would consider normal or even tolerable. He will have to subject himself to unending misery to eek out a few months of suffering before he finally succumbs. He should be angry, or sad, or desperate, or at the end of his ability to process intellectually. Instead, he sits calmly, absorbs the news with about as much emotion as we might expect from someone who has just heard the weather report for a land far away.

Governor Michael Dukakis

There is precedent for such a stunning lack of emotional response. During the 1988 presidential campaign, the Democratic Party nominee, Michael Dukakis, was seen by many as a wooden, emotionally detached man not fit to govern. In the first debate of the campaign, Bernard Shaw, then the CNN prime time news anchor, articulated one of the most famous questions ever put to a presidential candidate:

Bernard Shaw: Governor, if Kitty Dukakis [Gov. Dukakis' wife] were raped and murdered, would you favor an irrevocable death penalty for the killer?
Gov. Dukakis: No, I don't, Bernard, and I think you know I've opposed the death penalty during all of my life ... ah ... I don't see any evidence that it's a deterrent and I think there are better and more effective ways to deal with violent crime. We've done so in my own state and it's one of the reasons why we have had the biggest drop in crime in any industrial state in America ...

It is a common belief that people listen not so much for what is said but the way in which it is said. This was certainly true of popular reaction to Governor Dukakis' response to the rape question. The question itself should have struck him as offensive, unfair, and not worthy of dignified response. He should have been shocked that anyone would pose such a question. Instead, he responded with less emotion than one would expect from the HAL 9000. No one wanted a robot sitting in the Oval Office; Dukakis' wooden, insensitive, **inhuman** response to this question is cited as one of the main reasons for his defeat in November, 1988.

I am going to return in later essays to a deeper discussion of Walter's lack of emotion. But Walter's disconcerting emotional detachment is only one of the unsettling features of this passage in the pilot episode. We also have to grapple with his decision to withhold vital information from the person presumably closer to him than anyone else in the world: his wife, Skyler White.

The Separation of Church and State

Thomas Jefferson, letter to the Danbury Baptist Assn., 1 January 1802

We see from the very beginning of Breaking Bad that Walter White maintains an impenetrable wall not only around his emotions but around any feature of his life he might consider personal. At this early point in the series I serve no one by providing my take on Walter's psychological state and the underlying scientific reasons for his strange, inhuman behavior. But we can discuss the ramifications of his withdrawal.

First, we need to understand that Walter's decision to withhold from Skyler his diagnosis of terminal cancer was not a choice many married couples would consider to fall in the range of personal discretion. Walter was morally obliged to inform his wife of his condition because her legal, financial, and emotional wellbeing would be irrevocably affected by his slow death due to disease. It is precisely in situations such as these that a married person ceases to have personal autonomy. The marriage contract Walter voluntarily signed sixteen or seventeen years ago stipulated exactly this concession of freedom as a condition of married life.

Walter will insist throughout the remainder of the series on the justifiable beneficence of maintaining a rigid wall of separation between his personal, criminal endeavors and his public, family life. It will become the White family's "separation of church and state."

Regardless of the psychological determinants of his mental state, Walter somehow has the ability to rationalize the withholding of personal information, even when he is under moral or ethical obligation to share his knowledge. This ability has immediate bearing on the story, especially regarding his decision to keep his illegal activities secret from everyone. Vince Gilligan is not the first writer to develop a protagonist with the ability to live in a world he holds secret from everyone around him. Several of Walter's character traits are found in earlier works of fiction. I feel our understanding of Walter will benefit from a brief examination of three of these literary predecessors, all of them drawn from the interwar period of the 1930s.

Mr. Chips

Honoring the Teachers of America
United States Post Office, 1957 PD

Goodbye Mr. Chips is a 1934 novel by James Hilton, perhaps best known for his story of Shangri La in the novel *Lost Horizon*. Probably few people, though, can identify the protagonist of Lost Horizon, Hugh Conway, while the name 'Mr. Chips' has so permeated modern culture that most everyone can recite the essential facets of the fictional man's character.

Charles Edward Chipping, Mr. Chips, was a failure in the classroom until he met the person who changed his entire outlook on life, Katherine Bridges. Katherine instilled in Mr. Chips a sense of humor and fundamentally converted him from the hapless stick-in-the-mud he had been. Thanks to Katherine, Mr. Chips was able to relate to his students in ways no other teacher could.

Goodbye Mr. Chips is not so much the portrait of a teacher as it is the examination of an extraordinarily empathetic human being. His greatest demonstrations of level-headed compassion and charm occur not in the classroom, but in ordinary life. He is depicted as possessing not only empathy, but a courage of heart unique in his world, conditioned not by culture or society, but by the dictates of fundamental humanity. In one of the most moving passages of the novel, Mr. Chips publicly recites the names of fallen alumni of Brookfield who had only recently died in the First World War. To the astonishment of almost everyone present, he includes in his recitation the name of a former German colleague who had died fighting in the Kaiser's army.

We see already that Mr. Chips' life moved in quite a different direction from the route pursued by Walter White. But the influences on Mr. Chips were very different, too. The foremost influence in his life, his wife Katherine, allowed him to become more of a man than he had been prior to her interventions. This positive effect is exactly the opposite of Skyler's influence on Walter's life. We also see in the life of Mr. Chips no "separation of church and state" between his personal and public behavior. Mr. Chips is an open book, not a top-secret vault.

It is for these and related reasons that I believe we need to move beyond Charles Chipping to more completely appreciate Walter White. I believe two other 1930s characters, from works by philosophically opposed authors, must be considered if we have any hope of understanding the true origins of Walter White.

The Secret Life of Walter Mitty

The Secret Life of Walter Mitty, a 1939 novel by James Thurber, is probably more familiar in its later incarnation as a Danny Kaye movie of the same name, released in 1947. The name Walter Mitty is synonymous with the idea of an incapable person who daydreams of himself in heroic roles, or an individual who tries to pass himself off as someone he is not.

In Thurber's novel, Walter Mitty has five daydreams while driving his wife into town to go shopping and have her hair done at the beauty salon. He dreams of being a Navy pilot, a brilliant surgeon, a conniving assassin, a Royal Air Force pilot volunteering for a suicide mission, and finally that same pilot standing before a firing squad.

Danny Kaye in *The Secret Life of Walter Mitty*
Unknown artist, publicity trailer, 1947, PD

Like Walter White, Walter Mitty is married to a domineering wife who imposes her will on her husband with the expectation that he will accept her dictates without question. Like the later Walter, Thurber's protagonist erects a firm, thick wall between public life with his wife and the private world of his daydreams.

Walter Mitty is much closer in character and behavior to Walter White than the more frequently invoked Mr. Chips. In fact, it seems to me unlikely that Vince Gilligan created the character of Walter White without direct reference to Walter Mitty.

We recognize two important differences immediately. The first is that Walter Mitty's flights of fancy contain none of the darkness associated with Walter White's embrace of criminal and immoral activity. Walter Mitty inhabits his secret world not as a criminal but as a hero whose exploits would be celebrated by everyone. Walter White's secret activities, on the other hand, would serve as just cause for imprisonment or execution.

Second, Walter Mitty's life is unexceptional—we might even say boring. Walter White's life is about as far from boring as one could imagine. Doomed to die in a year or two, a surprise baby on the way, and no resources to pay for any of the treatment regimes he might undergo, Walter White would love to have even one boring option. Instead, any choice he could reasonably make is fraught with uncertainty, pain, and death.

There is a 1930s fictional character who flirted with danger and death, whose range of life choices never included boring options, and whose story exuded only darkness and psychological pain. I believe *The Short Happy Life of Francis Macomber* is the most natural starting point for a contemplation of the origins of Walter White.

Ernest Hemingway's Francis Macomber

Ernest Hemingway, Paris, 1924
Unknown photographer, 1924, PD

Ernest Hemingway considered himself among the "Lost Generation" (la génération perdue)—those of the age who had fought in the First World War, who bore the weight of the world on their shoulders without receiving their due. The world of Ernest Hemingway and Gertrude Stein abided neither by rhyme nor reason, and the human inability to contend with fickle nature is on full display in their literary style, called modernism.

In Hemingway's short story, *The Short Happy Life of Francis Macomber*, the titular protagonist is outwardly strong but inside fully a coward, similar in many ways to Walter White. He struggles with nature, in the form of the wild beasts of Africa, and fails to win the early battles. He collects a lion trophy only because of the intervention of his guide, Robert Wilson. Bagging the lion is the proof of manhood, and just as Walter White failed to "bring home the bacon," Francis Macomber failed to get the lion. Francis, like Walter, is being "dicked around," especially by Wilson, the guide, who is sleeping with Francis' wife.

Like Skyler, Francis' wife, Margot, rules over him and prevents the full expression of his masculine nature. Margot seems almost a force of nature herself, which for Hemingway means she must inevitably win any confrontation involving Francis.

The climax of the story has Francis finally standing his ground against a charging buffalo, shooting at it even as it comes within range of goring him. But just as he is about to enjoy the crown of full manhood, his wife, from the distant car, shoots—presumably at the buffalo—and the bullet pierces Francis' skull. Francis dies on the spot.

Francis could never win, of course, because modernism denied tidy and happy outcomes.

These modernist ideas are important to our consideration of Breaking Bad. At some point we need to pose the question of accountability. Is Walter White alone to blame for his decision to break bad, or do we need to take into account social forces and "acts of God"? Hemingway would have us place the blame on nature itself, and the individual human being's twisted relationship with the world. Even when Francis Macomber finally found courage inside his bones, he was denied the victory to which he was entitled. Could it be that Walter White is likewise doomed, that even if he acted courageously the forces of cruel and primal nature would break and destroy him?

I will not offer my own response to this fundamental question—not yet, anyway. I do not hesitate out of deference to your sensibilities as viewer-participant, but rather out of my bias as a novelist. I believe we do a disservice to Vince Gilligan and his writing team, and ultimately therefore to ourselves, if we attempt to force Breaking Bad into the narrow confines of one literary style or another. I believe any attempt to categorize Breaking Bad as an example of existing thought systems is convenient but ultimately short-sighted and illegitimate. Convenient, because it sure is easy to treat a television show as a paint-by-numbers endeavor that fits into pre-existing literary templates. Illegitimate, because the driving force behind Breaking Bad cannot be the will to demonstrate the superiority of a thought system. Breaking Bad must stand on its own internal merits, and not be forced to stoop to someone else's way of interpreting Walter White.

What I do offer here is an alternative way of looking at the relationship between nature and humans, using precisely the same imagery invoked by Hemingway. The intention is to show that Hemingway's vision is not uniquely valid. We have license to apply any interpretive pattern we favor.

A Bull Moose's Victory

Ernest Hemingway knew of at least one man who had never run from a charging buffalo, or even a ferocious lion. Theodore Roosevelt was a man's man and a hero to every boy born between 1885 and 1910. The courageous colonel who had created the Rough Riders and led the charge on San Juan Hill (for which he was posthumously awarded the Congressional Medal of Honor), the take-no-prisoners President of the United States who "spoke softly but carried a big stick," the diplomat who won the Nobel Peace Prize, and the naturalist and big game hunter who always bagged his prey, Theodore Roosevelt proved himself time and again equal to any challenge.

Theodore Roosevelt
African Game Trails, 1910

What's more, Theodore Roosevelt was a self-made man, at every level of his being. Born underweight and frail, TR was diagnosed early with severe asthma. He was so weak doctors advised that he be kept at home and not allowed to mingle with other children. He should be given at least a fighting chance of making it through childhood, though most believed he would die before his teenage years.

As soon as Roosevelt could think, he forced himself into a strict and exhausting routine of physical exercise. "Make your own body," he told himself, and through an unyielding regime of vigorous exercise and outdoor living, he transformed himself from dying invalid to arguably the most robust man of his generation. He climbed mountains, hiked in rain and snow, and generally confronted any obstacle with zeal.

Roosevelt's robust physique was not the stuff of fanciful tales, but hard reality. On October 14, 1912, Roosevelt was campaigning in Milwaukee, Wisconsin. Exiting his car to enter the arena where he was to speak, he was confronted by John Schrank, who fired his revolver at point plank range into Roosevelt's chest. The Bull Moose refused medical treatment. He went into Milwaukee Auditorium and gave a speech lasting 80 minutes. He did finally agree to medical treatment after the speech, but he didn't want the doctors fishing around in his chest. The bullet was never extracted from his body. He got a good night's sleep and continued campaigning the next day. Surviving a shot that would have killed most men, he suffered not much more than a momentary inconvenience to his campaign schedule.

Modernist Envy?

We know that Ernest Hemingway compared himself to Roosevelt, and found himself lacking. This is the biting poem Hemingway wrote shortly after TR's death in 1919:

Roosevelt
Workingmen believed
He busted trusts,
And put his picture in their windows.
"What he'd have done in France!"
They said.
Perhaps he would--
He could have died
Perhaps,
Though generals rarely die except in bed,
As he did finally.
And all the legends that he started in his life
Live on and prosper,
Unhampered now by his existence.

The final thought of the poem is clear: Roosevelt's legend was always bigger than the lesser reality of the man, and now that he was dead his legend would (unjustly) grow larger.

All of this is just so much sour grapes. If anything, the legend could never portray the full reality of Roosevelt, the man's man. But Hemingway was intent on proving the man false. When he planned his big game hunting trip in Africa—following the same trails Roosevelt had blazed 23 years before—he hired Philip Percival, the very same man who had guided Roosevelt.

Philip Percival was the template for Hemingway's fictional foil, Robert Wilson. But who was the template for Francis Macomber?

Hemingway was a hunter. He surely realized, though, even after a few days of tracking big game, that he was no Theodore Roosevelt. Perhaps he unfairly painted himself as the cowardly Francis Macomber. Roosevelt, after all, had never had to struggle with the bottle, as Hemingway did all his adult life. Roosevelt may have grown up under an excessively cautious mother, as Hemingway had, but Roosevelt's mother never dressed Theodore in girl's dresses, as Ernest's mother had.

Ernest Hemingway was a man of his time, but he was not a modern only because that was the artistic route to follow at the time. He was a modern in outlook because of his own upbringing and his very personal acquaintance with inner shortcomings and the failure to achieve the level of manhood he so desperately sought.

I think it is difficult not to see Hemingway as an unfortunate slave to unhappy destiny. But I think it is equally difficult to see Roosevelt as anything other than a self-made man who conquered every difficulty nature threw in his path.

The question we must ask ourselves is simple: Is Walter White more like Theodore Roosevelt, or more like Ernest Hemingway, or has he blazed an entirely new trail?

Gandhi spinning
Birla House, Mumbai, 1942
Unknown photographer, PD

Mohandas Gandhi On Homespun Cloth (called 'Khadi' in India)
If we have the 'khadi spirit' in us, we would surround ourselves with simplicity in every walk of life. The 'khadi spirit' means illimitable patience ... The 'khadi spirit' means also an equally illimitable faith ... illimitable faith in truth and non-violence ultimately conquering every obstacle in our way. The 'khadi spirit' means fellow-feeling with every human being on earth. It means a complete renunciation of everything that is likely to harm our fellow creatures, and if we but cultivate that spirit amongst the millions of our countrymen, what a land this India of ours would be!
—Mohandas K. Gandhi, *Young India*, 22 September 1927

Prologue II

[Xe]4f^{14}5d^{4}6s^{2}

The color white can mean many things. For the Mahatma Gandhi, white was a potent political symbol which he wielded to great effect against his philosophical adversaries, the colonial authorities of Great Britain.

The image of Walter White wearing only a green shirt and "tighty-whitey" jockey underwear in the New Mexico desert is burned into our memories. We have the feeling that the white jockey briefs are meant to convey greater significance than that of a simple undergarment, but what is that significance?

Colors are strong motifs throughout Breaking Bad. They carry raw symbolic power intended to mold our thinking about characters and their actions. As with most motifs in Breaking Bad, however, the correspondence between symbol and the idea it expresses is never static. Good guys wear both black and white, and every color in between. Bad guys are as likely to wear pink and yellow as they are to vest themselves in blue or black. How do we discern symbolic meaning when the symbols themselves are constantly changing?

Many have attempted a color analysis of Breaking Bad. "Red is the color of violence," we are told by one self-appointed expert. "Pink is the color of death," another proclaims, after she views the final episode of Season Two. With all due respect to these wannabe authorities, I disagree with their assessment. If red always represents violence in Breaking Bad, when we see Junior wearing bright red boxer underwear are we to believe that he is a seething bundle of rage, just waiting for the opportunity to kill the next person who insults him?

The connection between colors and the ideas they represent is fluid, varying from situation to situation and from one character to another. Over the course of five years we will see Walter White wearing clothing of just about every hue and shade imaginable. Nevertheless, it is possible to discern certain dominant trends and such is my intention in this chapter.

The Gandhian Example

The Mahatma's Satyagraha Salt March in 1930 had as its final result the production of pure white salt, a symbol of India's determination to gain political and economic freedom from British overlords.

Great Father Gandhi on the Satyagraha Salt March
Unknown photographer, March, 1930, PD

Salt had political and economic significance at the time because Indians were legally bound to pay a salt tax to the British Empire. By walking to the sea with the intention of making salt and then using it without paying the tax, Gandhiji was breaking British colonial law.

We could certainly understand white salt to symbolize the purity of Indian aspirations toward independent statehood. My impression, after studying the saint's march, his declarations during that march, and independence movement activity around that time, is that salt was more than anything a symbol of Indian unity. In essence, salt became the Great Father's way of proclaiming that India was already a state, already independent at heart, and it remained only for the less-than-observant British to recognize the fact of Indian independence.

As important as salt was, though, I have to believe Gandhi's most effective political weapon was probably the homespun cloth (khadi) he made himself, spinning yarn on wheels he built, transforming the yarns into cloth he weaved on hand-made looms. He famously wore a single white covering, often referred to as a "loincloth" (though the garment covered him from navel to knee). Winston Churchill detested Gandhi, referring to him as a "half-naked fakir."

The symbolic essence of the Mahatma's "loincloth" becomes obvious after only a brief acquaintance with the saint's writing on the subject. In the Richard Attenborough film biography, the Mahatma is depicted at a resistance rally, encouraging the hundreds of thousands listening to him to burn their British-made garments:

> English factories make the cloth – that makes our poverty. All those who wish to make the English see, bring me the cloth from Manchester and Leeds that you wear tonight, and we will light a fire that will be seen in Delhi – and London! And if, like me, you are left with only one piece of homespun – wear it with dignity!

I don't know that the final statement, "If, like me, you are left with only one piece of homespun—wear it with dignity" is an authentic quote, but in the end it doesn't matter. The words accurately convey Gandhi's thought about Indian-made cloth. Homespun, or 'khadi,' was again a symbol of Indian unity, but it also became a Gandhian symbol of Indian and human dignity. One could not feel dignified wearing clothing that enslaved its wearer, but one would feel the complete liberating weight of dignity in consciously deciding to wear garments made by friend and neighbor.

Walter's Essence

The Indian saint's loincloth and the meth manufacturer's jockey underwear are both white, both undergarments, both representative of something essential to the person.

Jesse: Those [Pointing to Walter's jockey underwear as Walter removes his green shirt] Wow. Those … ah … you're keepin' those on, right?

Walter [Turning to face Jesse, stares at him for a moment, sighs] Come on. [Enters the RV]

Walter won't take off the white jockey shorts. He seems disgusted that Jesse would even ask the question. But the question appears valid to us as viewer-participants, too. It is hard to imagine a less dignified image than that of a high school teacher in the New Mexico desert, stripping to his underwear so he can manufacture crystalline methamphetamine. The image is so incongruous, in fact, that we find ourselves laughing. Breaking Bad is categorized as "black comedy," after all, and this highly memorable scene is one of the first of hundreds that will have us chuckling or even rolling on the floor.

We can be certain that the "tighty-whiteys" do not represent Walter's dignity. He lost any semblance of dignity when he removed his shirt and slacks. He did not seem at all concerned about modesty. It is not difficult for me to imagine Walter White going skinny dipping with Skyler or perhaps even with college buddies. I really doubt that simple modesty played any role in his decision to retain the jockey shorts. The reality of cable television and its legal limitations might normally apply in our thinking, but only moments before in the pilot episode we were witness to a topless woman whose breasts were blurred out by editors. If it had been important that Walter remove his underwear, we can be sure the editors would have blurred out his nudity—or not. We will see at least two scenes later in the series in which Walter's naked backside appears without any editorial blurring.

But Walter kept his underwear on throughout the remainder of the episode. The decision was conscious, and the imagery was intended to carry bold, symbolic significance. The white jockey underwear was intended to represent to us an essential aspect of Walter's character—something he would not surrender, even if he gave up his dignity and every shred of any other human quality we might believe him to possess. The white underwear, then, is symbolic of something Walter will not give up, no matter the situation or the personal cost to him.

What is the one essential aspect of Walter White's character that he refuses to give up?

Purity as Metaphor

We see intentionally chosen white garments in several situations throughout the series. In Season One, this choice is most evident in the meth manufacturing sequences. Both Walter and Jesse are depicted wearing white Tyvek clean room garments. This costume decision by the Breaking Bad production team is interesting for a number of reasons.

Seagate's Clean Room

First, garments of the type Walter and Jesse wear during meth synthesis are typically required only in the final stages of manufacture. Yet we see both characters wearing the suits during the entire synthesis routine. An amateur meth manufacturer would use any clothing he liked, but the idea here is that Walter White is no amateur meth manufacturer. He is applying fundamental chemical principles and top flight technical expertise to the manufacture of high-purity drug product rivaling the quality of anything available through FDA-approved pharmaceutical processes.

The reality as I have experienced it is a bit different than what is portrayed onscreen. I have worked in the major types of pharmaceutical manufacture as consulting scientist or co-creator of processes. In the synthetic processes I have developed the full splash suits we see Walter and Jesse wearing are usually not specified until the penultimate and final steps of a process. The PPE (personal protective equipment) used in the early steps of a process would be determined by the safety concerns posed by the chemicals and the limitations of the manufacturing equipment. It is unlikely, indeed, that a pharmaceutical process would require hours-long respirator ("gas mask") usage; any such requirement would likely be due to the inadequacy of the manufacturing process. But I have collaborated in creating FDA-approved processes that require workers to wear respirators for the full eight or twelve hour shift, too, due to extraordinary process requirements that could not be relieved by practical manufacturing system upgrades.

The safety concerns in the penultimate and final steps of the process are superseded by product integrity concerns. Full Tyvek "space suits" are *de rigueur* even in final operations in which there is practically zero safety concern for the workers. The intention in the penultimate and final operations is to prevent even the slightest contamination of product, and the most likely source of contamination, by far, is the workers themselves. In early steps of the process a simple hairnet to keep hair out of the product may suffice, but in the final step the workers will wear a hairnet underneath the hood, and the entire face may be covered, not for worker protection, but to keep hair and even the smallest particle of dry skin out of the product.

My first impression on viewing these scenes, as a pharmaceutical chemist, is **overkill**. Walter and Jesse are wearing the wrong type of PPE at the wrong time. My first impression, as a hack writer with authority-level expertise in pharmaceutical process development, is that the clothing has been chosen not to demonstrate fidelity with pharmaceutical manufacturing norms, but to make a symbolic or metaphorical statement.

I am very comfortable coming to this conclusion regarding the rationale for putting Jesse and Walter in white Tyvek in Seasons One and Two. First of all, Vince Gilligan hired top-rate industry experts to advise him on the nitty-gritty technical details of pharmaceutical and methamphetamine manufacture. Second, a very intentional change in laboratory garment color was made later in the series for symbolic reasons. Third, as a writer, I know something about "how the sausage is made," and the tasty sausage we enjoy as viewer-participants is often delivered with heavy doses of flavor-enriched symbolism and metaphor, even if delivering that symbolism means we have to depart a bit from realism.

The cover of the *Breaking Blue* provides an example of a storyteller's concession to symbolism. If I had wished to deliver a realistic portrayal of a pharmaceutical manufacturer holding a handful of blue methamphetamine I would have depicted a hand covered with a blue or purple 3-mil nitrile glove. These are the gloves used in industry, and they are the gloves faithfully portrayed in Breaking Bad. But I had to accomplish several artistic goals. The blue meth had to stand out as the focal point of the image, and that was virtually impossible if the glove holding the meth was also blue. Using instead a yellow nitrile glove (which was a major research undertaking—*I found only one manufacturer of yellow nitrile gloves in the world!*) made sense, because the yellow glove would also help me with a second objective, which was to emphasize the symbolic importance of the color yellow in Breaking Bad.

But I had two even greater objectives. The title of my major Breaking Bad book is *Breaking Blue*. Bringing attention to the blue meth as focal point was paramount because the final goal of this book is to reveal the symbolic importance and meaning of the color blue in Breaking Bad. Finally, the gloved hand, held in precisely the same way as the hand holding the two stones on the cover of *LOST Humanity* (my first book on the television series *Lost*), would project imagery I have been associating with my pen name, Pearson Moore. When readers see a hand held out this way on a book cover, I want them to think, "Oh, a Pearson Moore book."

Purity as Revelation of Self

The Transfiguration
Carl Heinrich Bloch, circa 1880

Many impressions pop through our heads when we see these men in their white clean room chemical suits: Professionalism, technical prowess, scientific excellence, manufacturing integrity—but probably the first thing that comes to mind is ***purity***. Walter White's methamphetamine is beyond compare in quality and physiological effect because it is absolutely pure.

Jesse: This is glass grade ... I mean you got ... Jesus, you got crystals in here two inches three inches long. [Turning to Walter] This is pure glass.
Walter:[nods]
Jesse: You're a damn artist. This is art, Mr White.

Jesse says this in the pilot episode, when Walter is "cooking" in white jockey underwear and black apron. It is only in later episode that we see Walter in the full white Tyvek suit.

Gilligan has thrown plenty of red herrings onto the path toward an understanding of the color white. "White is the color of vanilla, of blandness," he said during an interview in early 2011 (Interview by Mike Flaherty, Vulture.com, 16 May 2011). Walter frequently appears dressed only in his jockey underwear to serve as biting humor. In the introduction to Episode 1.04, for instance, Hank describes the unusual expertise of some new players in the meth market:

Now, we don't know who they are or where they come from, but they possess an extremely high skill set. Personally, I'm thinkin' Albuquerque might just have a new kingpin.

As Hank is talking, the visual switches to Walter, dressed only in his white jockey shorts, brushing his teeth. How could someone so 'vanilla,' so *bland,* be "a new kingpin"? The idea is preposterous, and the juxtaposition of Hank's speech extoling the "high skill set" with Walter brushing his teeth in his underwear is high cinematic art.

But we know the color white does not mean 'bland,' and we know the virtue associated with Walter's jockey underwear is not "an extremely high skill set" in meth making. The metaphorical purity of Walter is not defined by his mastery of chemistry. "Actually it's just basic chemistry," Walter says in the pilot episode in response to Jesse's praise. "But thank you, Jesse, I'm glad it's acceptable."

If white does not mean 'bland' and it does not mean "extremely high skill set," what does it mean?

The Unbearable Grayness of Being

We receive another red herring (ah … *white* herring?) in Episode 1.05, Gray Matter. Badger is dressed almost entirely in white. He juggles glass bottles in the RV, stuffs Cheetos up his nose, and generally behaves in a manner unbecoming. So is white perhaps the color of buffoonery? Wouldn't all of Walter's early appearances in white jockey underwear fit perfectly as symbolic representations of a competent man who has turned himself into a clown?

The image of Badger dressed in white, behaving as an undisciplined jester, ought to fit, but it does not. Jesse and Badger are, after all, best friends. We could easily imagine Jesse, a day or a week before meeting Walter White 'professionally,' behaving in the same childish manner as Badger. But something has changed inside Jesse.

"Wow," Badger says, in awe of Jesse's knowledge of chemical glassware, "you really know your shit." Jesse smiles and shrugs. "It's just basic chemistry," he says, parroting the words Walter used only days before. So the fact is, it's not "just basic chemistry." The fact that Walter made meth of incomparable quality and Jesse knows (or *thinks* he knows) the proper technical terms for various types of glassware is not inconsequential. It is fundamental to Walter, and fundamental to Jesse.

White and black make gray. This is the basis for the multi-billion-dollar company Walter, Elliott, and Gretchen started some 20 years before. Walter's last name is White, Elliott's last name is Schwartz, which is German for *Black*. Thus, when they formed their company, the three founders (Walter White, *his* girlfriend Gretchen, and his friend Elliott Schwartz) named their entrepreneurial creation Gray Matter Technologies.

How do I know Gretchen was Walter's girlfriend (or possibly fiancée)? Look at the way they interact with each other in the introduction to Episode 1.03. Walter and Gretchen are not acquaintances. The way he touches her while they're talking, the close proximity of their bodies, the way they look at each other—they are more than friends.

Why would he give her up, to his best friend, no less? Why would he give up his share in the company, a company he founded with his own sweat through extraordinary technical abilities that led him to become "Contributor to Research Awarded the Nobel Prize"?—a company now worth billions of dollars? What could be worth so much to Walter White that he would forego a life of pampered luxury, a salary of millions of dollars per year? Why would he decide, in essence, that White could not be mixed with anything else, that he would not surrender White to become Gray?

At Elliott's birthday party (1.05) Skyler revealed Walter's diagnosis of terminal cancer. Elliott first offered Walter a job, "Yes, kind of like some fig leaf, you know, some face-saving bullshit that allowed me to generously accept his charity."

Skyler: Okay, what did you say? Walt?
Walter: What do you think I said?
Skyler: Why? Walt!

Walter did not respond to Skyler's question. We got our answer, though, moments later in the New Mexico desert, from Walter's protegé, Jesse Pinkman.

Purity and Prejudice

Superbia
Pieter Bruegel the Elder, 1557

Jesse has spent a day and a half in the RV trying to synthesize meth meeting his new standards. He picks up a nearly perfect crystal with tweezers. His friend, Badger, marvels at the product.

Badger: You are a genius, bro. This [stuff] is unreal. When I get back I'm gonna burn that dollar bill ... 'cause we're gonna make some mad dough!

Jesse: [Examining the crystal] It's not right. [He's upset]

Badger: What do you mean it's not right?

Jesse: It's … cloudy. It's not supposed to be cloudy, okay, that last time it was glass.

Badger: So what? Cloudy, not cloudy? It looks good enough to me!"

Jesse: [nods, sighs] "Good enough." [He picks up the tray of meth, goes out the door]

Badger: Yo! What are you doing?

Jesse: [walks eight steps away from the RV, throws the trayful of meth into the air.]

Badger: AGH!! Are you out of your mind? I totally would have smoked that!

Jesse: Look, it's not for you, it's for our customers. They're going to demand a certain standard.

Badger: WHAT?! What? What are you? WHAT?!

Jesse: We'll just do it again, until we get it right.

Jesse's customers are "going to demand a certain standard." The statement would have made more sense to Badger if Jesse had formed the words in Sanskrit, or Swahili. Badger was probably more discriminating that any of Jesse's potential customers. He had held a job and he was occasionally able to speak in full sentences that could be deciphered into some semblance of Standard English. But Jesse's words constituted the most insufferably obtuse declaration Badger had ever heard.

Jesse's customers have no 'standards.' As he will say later, in Episode 3.10, "We make poison for people who don't care." Even those among us who have never tried Jesse's product understand the appropriateness of Badger's response to Jesse's rationale for throwing out perfectly good product. Jesse's action would be stunning to any reasonable observer. We know there is absolutely no connection between the quality of Jesse's product and his customers' 'standards.'

It took Vince Gilligan five episodes to define the meaning of the single garment Walter White would never surrender. In the end, it was the character who is the moral center of the series who spelled it out for us:

Alright, look at it this way, okay. It's the bottom of the ninth, bases are loaded, you're up. But you got a bum arm, alright? There's no frickin' way you're gonna hit a homer, okay? So you can either let the *pinch hitter* take the bat, or you can hold onto your pride and lose the game. Get what I'm sayin'?

No one in the room understands Hank's baseball analogy—except us. The 'pinch hitter,' the guy who will step in for Walter, is Elliott Schwartz. Hank means to say Walter doesn't have the financial resources to win against cancer, so Walter should allow Elliott Schwartz to pay for his treatment.

You got your pride, man. I get it. Okay, I get it. But if Daddy Warbucks wants to chip in, man, I'm with your old lady on this one. I say take the money and run, man.

All things considered, with Walter's responsibilities as father, husband, and high school chemistry teacher, his priorities are out of line, Hank is saying. Pride is important. But pride is not the most important element in a well-lived life.

Hank discovered the essential core of Walter, the aspect of his brother in law's inner self that he will not surrender, never compromise (never allow White to be compromised into Gray), never remove from his person even when he has given up everything else that others may consider essential to life as a fully expressed human being.

White, in Breaking Bad, is symbolic of PRIDE.

This may not be true for other characters, but it is true for Walter White. Pride is so important to Walter that he was willing to give up his girlfriend, give up his company, give up the opportunity to enjoy a life on Easy Street—and now, two decades later, he is willing to give up his very life rather than surrender his pride.

Walter didn't remove his white jockey shorts during that first day of cooking because it symbolized the core value motivating every choice he has ever made in his life.

Some will say he is entitled. Give me liberty or give me death. Live free or die. Didn't Walter's ancestors fight a war with Great Britain over these very ideas? Isn't pride the greatest of virtues which a fully alive human being might jealously guard in daily life, as a matter of principle, as possibly the supreme expression of human life?

Jesse: Tell me why you're doing this, seriously.
Walter: Why do you do it?

Jesse: Money, mainly.

Walter:There you go. [Walks away]

Jesse: Naw. Come on, man. Some straight like you, giant stick up his ass, all of a sudden age—what? Sixty? He's just gonna break bad?

Walter:I'm fifty.

Jesse: It's weird, is all, okay. It doesn't compute. Listen, if you've gone crazy or something, I mean, if you've gone crazy—or depressed—I'm just sayin' that's something I need to know about, okay? I mean, that affects me.

Walter:I am awake.

Indeed. Walter is awake, maybe for the first time in his life. Even if he did end up surrendering his pride in little ways after he gave up Gray Matter, he will never do so again. Not even in little ways. Walter White is fully awake. He will wield his pride as the most lethal weapon ever depicted on a television series. Eventually all of his philosophical adversaries will fall to the power of his symbolic weapon—unless, of course, there is in the Breaking Bad universe a symbolic virtue of greater power than pride. Is there, after all, a more important element in a well-lived life?

Michael Faraday's Christmas Lecture
Alexander Blaikley, circa 1856

Chemistry is—well, technically, chemistry is the study of matter. But I prefer to see it as the study of change.

—Walter Hartwell White, Chemistry Lecture
(Episode 1.01)

Chapter H

High School
Chemistry Teacher

"The chemistry must be respected."

Walter White might have uttered this declaration anytime during Season One, but the words did not actually depart his lips until Season Three (3.05). Breaking Bad certainly "respects the chemistry" both literally and figuratively. The show has elevated chemistry to become the metaphorical backbone of the show, and accomplished this without requiring any knowledge of chemistry on the part of viewer-participants.

'Chemistry' and 'Teacher' are essential themes in Breaking Bad, and we will frequently return to these ideas in later essays. Walter's formal classroom lectures are placed low on his daily priority list, but he is methodical and conscientious in his approach to mentoring Jesse, and their teacher-student relationship will only grow in importance in coming seasons.

If chemistry acts as the storyteller's center, and if the student-teacher relationship is the concept that places characters in proper relation to each other, the idea of 'high school' is foundational to Walter's character and the decision he makes to break bad. Understanding the connection between Walter's vocation and the trigger events and conditions is important to our deeper enjoyment of Breaking Bad.

I will touch on all three concepts (chemistry, teacher, high school) in this essay, with particular emphasis on chemistry. I will address chemistry as a technical discipline, to be sure (I am a professional chemist, after all!), but I will devote the bulk of this chapter to an examination of chemistry's importance to Walter's personal life and the manner in which he prioritizes his thoughts, actions, and time.

Pearson Moore

Chemistry 101: Observation

Walter White's first chemistry lesson (1.01) was not much different from the first lesson many of us received in high school.

Chemistry—it is the study of … what? Anyone? Chemistry is—well, technically, chemistry is the study of matter. But I prefer to see it as the study of change. Now just think about this. Electrons, they change their energy levels. Molecules: molecules change their bonds. Elements: they combine and change into compounds. Well, that's all of life, right?

Envisioning chemistry as the study of change is the natural bias of Breaking Bad. Walter White, after all, must eventually be transformed from Mr. Chips (or Walter Mitty or Francis Macomber) into Scarface. But designating chemistry as the study of change makes sense from a practical, technical point of view, too. My first chemistry teacher, Frederick P. Buechler, impressed this point upon our class by giving each student a candle and a box of matches for our first lesson. "Record your observations about these two objects, but be sure you record only observations, not conclusions." Now, you wouldn't think that the observation of a candle flame could be all that interesting, but you'd be wrong.

Mr. Buechler: Stand up and tell the class your observations about the two objects.
Student: When we lit the wick, the candle started burning.
Mr. Buechler: You "lit the wick"? How?
Student: With the match.
Mr. Buechler: [Takes an unlit match from the box, touches it to the candle wick. Nothing happens] Like that?
Student: [Laughing] No, the match was lit.
Mr. Buechler: 'Lit'?
Student: I mean the match was burning.
Mr. Buechler: What does 'burning' mean?
Student: [Confers with another student, faces front, smiling] It was oxidizing.
Mr. Buechler: Oh ho! Oxidizing. Do you mean the cellulose of the match was reacting with molecular oxygen from the atmosphere, leading to the sustained generation of light energy and the production of carbon dioxide and water through oxidation?

Student: [Frowning, perplexed] Yeah, I guess.

Mr. Buechler: No, sorry. Those are conclusions, not observations. Now, if you had told me you struck the match head on the side of the box, you **saw** flames, you **heard** a sizzling noise, you **smelled** a sulphurous odor, you **felt** heat from the flame—*those* are observations.

Sherlock Holmes
D. H. Friston, 1887

The two hours Mr. Buechler devoted to the study of a candle were the most important two hours of my career as a chemist. Good chemists, Mr. Buechler taught us, are first of all good observers. As chemists, though, we have a natural bias in terms of wishing to observe, record, and make sense of *changes* in matter, just as Walter White told us in his first lesson. A red liquid

Pearson Moore

in a bottle and a blue liquid in a bottle are somewhat interesting, and we can characterize the physical properties of these two liquids, but in doing so we could be physicists or even psychologists, not necessarily chemists. But if we start with a red liquid in a bottle, do something to it (turn it upside down, heat it, pass it through sand, add a few crystals of something, or shake it—or whatever) and the color changes to blue, we are much more interested because change is what we enjoy observing (studying) as chemists.

Observation is important to us as viewer-participants, too. The extent to which we make observations, rather than injecting our conclusions (personal biases) into what we see and hear transpire on the screen, determines our ability to gather enough information to make sense of the show. At some point we will have to render judgment—we will have to make conclusions—but the longer we can make observations rather than formulate conclusions, the more we will become aware of important contributing factors to our analysis.

Thus, in the previous chapter I could have just started the essay by saying "The color white in Breaking Bad symbolizes pride," but in so doing I would have biased your analysis of data. You would have been searching for ways that a particular scene indicated pride, rather than considering the placement and interaction of elements within a scene and the full range of possible meanings. By delaying the statement until the end of the chapter, I invited you to make wide-ranging observations and come to your own conclusions. Quite likely you decided that the color white means something else—the comic unsuitability of a character's mindset in a given situation, perhaps, or the fundamental aspect of the character's inner self, or some other idea entirely. Any of those are fine, and I hope as you read these essays you will consider the ideas I bring to the fore as mere examples of ways to consider the show's deeper meaning. My analysis is not "right" or "better" than anyone else's examination of Breaking Bad.

The Meaning of Life

Walter White concluded his first chemistry lecture with a thought that will resonate throughout the five years of Breaking Bad. We know the words are important because they appear in the very first episode. Walter is addressing us directly:

[Chemistry] is all of life, right? It's the constant, it's the cycle, it's solution, dissolution, just over and over and over. It is growth, then decay, then transformation. It is fascinating, really.

Chemist Comedy, Mixed with a Bit of Island Humor
Pearson Moore 2012

So that there would be no confusion in our minds regarding the significance of Walter's statement, he made his understanding of the meaning of life clear in Episode 1.03, when his then-girlfriend, Gretchen, recited the molar quantities of each element making up the human body and Walter recorded them on the blackboard.

It was an interesting exercise in many ways. We think of life as being carbon-based, but as Gretchen's analysis showed, the human body contains far more hydrogen and oxygen atoms than it does carbon atoms. This, of course, is because humans are primarily composed of water, as Walter noted in passing ("Oxygen 26 [percent]—there you have your water"). Carbon makes up only nine percent of the human body, on a molar (number of atoms) basis.

The happy couple continued their analysis all the way through the trace elements, "down where the magic happens."

Walter:	So, the whole thing adds up to 99.888042%. We are 0.111958% shy.
Gretchen:	Supposedly that's everything.
Walter:	Yeah?
Gretchen:	Uh-huh.
Walter:	I don't know. I just … I just … just seems like something's missing, doesn't it? There's got to be more to a human being than that.

Episode 1.03 advanced the plot in significant ways, but it also reached into Walter to reveal one of the most important facts about his belief system. All of this was accomplished in the context of an extended meditation on the meaning of human life. It was in this episode that Walter had to decide whether to kill Krazy 8 or allow him to go free.

Walter's academic discussion with Gretchen regarding the nature of human life was juxtaposed with the nausea-inducing scene in which Jesse and Walter mopped, sponged, and squeegeed the liquid remains of Emilio Koyama into the toilet. Perhaps there was more to human life than hydrogen, oxygen, carbon, nitrogen, phosphorus, calcium, and sodium, but these are precisely the materials we saw Walter dump into the toilet. The repulsive scene made clear that nothing more than simple chemical compounds form the human body. The juxtaposition made clear the deeper truth that something much greater was at stake.

Walter wanted to believe there's more. "[It] just seems like something's missing, doesn't it?" His academic struggles took on life-and-death significance as he looked into the eyes of Krazy 8 and sought a reason to keep the young man alive. He agonized over the pros and cons of ending the life of his prisoner. Maybe to his surprise, he discovered several good reasons to spare Krazy 8's life. Among the many reasons Walter recorded on the Let Him Live side of the ledger:

It's the moral thing to do.
Judeo/Christian principles
You are not a murderer.
Sanctity of life—
Won't be able to live with yourself
Post-traumatic stress
Murder is wrong

The single entry on the Kill Him side of the ledger was striking and persuasive:

He'll kill your entire family if you let him go.

The cold calculus associated with this analysis seemed clear: Walter was obliged to kill Krazy 8.

The conclusion must have been clear to Walter, too, even if the thought of what he had to do was unthinkably disgusting. That he hesitated meant he was considering other possibilities. Perhaps he contemplated the possibility that human life cannot be quantified, that there is more to life than chemistry. He brought up moral concerns, after all, but what did these concerns really mean to Walter?

I think Walter was truly struggling with the morality of his decision. I believe in some way, perhaps unconsciously, he was attaching more than chemical significance to the human life he contemplated snuffing out.

Osiris Judging the Human Heart
Unknown artist, the Papyrus of Hunefer, circa 1375 B.C.

But I believe in the end he appealed to the scientific part of his mind to render the final verdict on Krazy 8's fate. The scientist would ask about the validity of conclusions. Perhaps, Walter might have thought, his conclusion was based on inadequate observation. Had his incomplete understanding of criminal life led him to jump to conclusions about what Krazy 8 would do to his family?

So Walter gathered more data. The fascinating aspect of his slow walk down to the basement is that his subconscious feeling that there was a spiritual value to human life was probably much stronger than the relatively feeble sense that he had inadequate information to render an informed decision. His conscience was weighing more heavily on his heart than his scientific self was weighing on his intellect, but he must have taken some degree of comfort in believing that he was merely gathering data for a particularly important experiment.

What he found in the course of his data collection is that Krazy 8 had a heart. He had a family, he cultivated wide-ranging interests, and he'd even studied at university. He was the son of a respected member of the community. He was well spoken, well studied, and calm in his bearing. Even if Walter had no hard data, everything about Krazy 8's civilized discourse and reasoned disposition appealed directly to Walter's moral sense. Walter decided the non-scientific evidence of the heart could not be denied. With a sense of resignation, then, and perhaps a good measure of relief, he returned upstairs to retrieve the key that would give Krazy 8 his freedom.

I think this was a critical point for Walter White. Possibly for the first time in his life he was allowing feeling, intuition, and conscience to guide a major life choice—in this case the decision to let Krazy 8 go free. If he had not thought to retrieve the broken ceramic plate from the trash, his life might have turned out quite differently. He might have made ethics the first consideration in any future decision. He might have been a happier man.

But Walter scooped up the pieces of the plate and put them together, and in that moment the full weight and unwavering constancy of the universe came crashing into his conscious awareness. Krazy 8 would, indeed, kill Walter's entire family.

The Universe

Walter had been willing to suspend and subsume to human compassion every scientific and logical lesson he had learned in his life. He had consented to surrender his intellect to his heart. Now, with the cold scientific evidence before him, in the brutal dishonesty of the missing shard, Walter's scientific training was vindicated, his worst fears confirmed. The Universe, Walter concluded, was telling him what his intellect had been telling him all along: You cannot trust Krazy 8. If you allow the psychopath to go free he will kill your entire family.

With Walter, I had the overwhelming sense in this scene that some unalterable aspect of life was intruding into Walter's interaction with the young meth distributor. But I think my perception of the unyielding nature of the Universe differed significantly from Walter's. I did not understand Walter's destiny to have been determined at that moment, but rather three days earlier, when he had made the decision to break bad. It was that earlier decision that forced Walter into the unpleasant Catch-22 predicament of choosing between his family's life and Krazy 8's life.

Even at that moment, though, staring at the broken pieces of ceramic plate on Jesse's kitchen table, Walter had more than two options. He could have gone to the police with his story. He could have fled with his family. He could have gone into business with Krazy 8, as he later did with Tuco.

The Soul Attains, Pygmalion
Edward Burne-Jones, 1870

I believe we need to understand the significance of this moment to Walter. He believed the Universe was confirming what he had believed all along: Human science and logic are the final judges of human value. As we learned in Episode 1.03, Walter had believed this all his life:

Walter: Just … doesn't it seem like something is missing?
Gretchen: What about the soul?
Walter: [Turns to look at Gretchen, laughs, walks toward her] The soul? [Brings his face to within three inches of hers] There's nothing but chemistry here.

The body language of Walter's last words to Gretchen in the university classroom indicated the double entendre: Chemistry referred to the material reality of the human body but also to the sexual attraction between Walter and Gretchen. More importantly, though, it confirmed any lack of spiritual sentiment in Walter's outlook. The human body was composed of chemical elements and sexual feeling, nothing more.

But juxtaposition was again used to tell us that the question was not settled in Walter's mind. As he sat in his car thinking on those words uttered 20 or more years in the past, he must have been wondering what had caused him to give up Gretchen. He was at a disadvantage here, in that he had to factor in the complexities of his relationship with the woman before and after their human body discussion in the empty classroom. Thanks to selective editing, we viewer-participants suffer no such limitations. The guiding force of Walter's life, his deference to the law of logic, was the aspect of his character that drove him away from Gretchen. She, in her open-minded appeal to Walter's spiritual essence, was willing to forgive his lack of spiritual self-knowledge. Walter, on the other hand, had to leave her, because he could not subscribe to any notion of spirituality. The fact that Walter was portrayed sitting in his car, meditating on the long-ago incident in the university classroom, can only mean that even though Walter doesn't realize it himself, he still is, in some sense, a spiritual being and not the collection of chemical elements and compounds he has believed all his life.

We will hear of this unseen character, The Universe, at critical moments in the next several seasons. For now, we may believe that chemistry stands outside of or subordinate to the overwhelming features of the unseen character. The genius of Vince Gilligan, though, is that he is going to bring chemistry back into the fold before the end of this series. All of it will make sense, even if now we must struggle with so many plot threads and character traits and trends and developments that we find ourselves confused. The descent of Walter White is clear. The reasons for his descent, and the symbolism attached to his fall, seem shrouded in dense mystery.

Some will say that Walter is a disciple of particular philosophical positions. Walter is a materialist, we are told. The problem with statements like this is that they give short shrift to scenes such as the one at the end of Episode 1.03, depicting Walter in a decidedly non-materialist contemplative state of mind. But the greater problem with the willy-nilly application of inadequate generalizations is that they are going to fall short of the full truth. By the end of the series it will not be pride or materialism *per se* that leads to the downfall of Walter White.

Walter's blindness to the full reality of human life and his determination to surrender his heart to his intellect prevented him from understanding what the Universe was telling him in the broken plate. We need to be better scientists than Walter. We need to refuse to ascribe his behavior to paradigms and theories and other black-and-white academic categories, because all of them will prove inadequate. Let us resolve to be good scientists. Let us observe and not arrive at hasty conclusions. Let's allow Walter to be Walter—or Heisenberg—and see where he takes us.

Science Teacher

Bill Nye the Science Guy
U.S. Dept. of Education, #ThankATeacher, 2012, PD

"The chemistry must be respected."

The words are spoken from a position of authority and they constitute excellent advice from chemistry teacher to pupil or protégé. Walter told Jesse to put Emilio's body into a polyethylene container. Jesse used ordinary logic to figure out that a solid porcelain bathtub must be superior in all ways to a flimsy blue plastic container. If hydrofluoric acid could "chemically disincorporate" a human body, what would it do to a thin plastic bin from a department store?

We witnessed the result of Jesse's 'logic' when the bathtub and floor underneath gave way to the inexorable corrosive power of hydrofluoric acid—used for over a century to etch glass, steel, ceramic, and yes, porcelain.

As an aside, for any would-be disincorporators out there, hydrofluoric acid is likely to violently incapacitate, render unconscious, cause permanent acute injury, and ultimately kill anyone attempting to use it in this manner. It is very unlikely to render and disincorporate any mammalian body—at least in the way depicted on the television show. There are cheap, effective, 100% chemical means of turning dead bodies into untraceable masses of gelatinized goop, but Breaking Bad isn't divulging that information, and I'm not, either. Likewise with the production of methamphetamine. If you pay close attention in the later episodes you will be able to discern a formula for the synthesis of methamphetamine. Good luck trying to apply it, though. You will end up with a useless mess if you attempt to duplicate Walter's Blue Sky formula.

A chemical reaction that Breaking Bad doesn't intentionally misrepresent is the thermite reaction:

$$Fe_2O_3 + 2\ Al \rightarrow 2\ Fe + Al_2O_3$$

The reaction unleashes torrents of light, heat, and sputtering, splattering gobs of molten, 4570 °F liquid metal, exactly as portrayed in the methylamine robbery sequence. In fact, the sputtering and splattering can be more severe than depicted, even with small amounts of thermite, and there's no way to stop the reaction. Water is worse than useless in a thermite fire, because spraying it on the burning material will only spread it around. Even sand would just turn into molten rock in the presence of thermite. There is a humorous video on Youtube in which a British television version of Mythbusters attempts to put out a thermite fire with liquid nitrogen, which will put out most any fire—but not a thermite reaction. The only thing accomplished by dousing with liquid nitrogen was to spread the red-hot liquid metal into a huge radius around the container.

Walter teaches this and many other lessons useful to practitioners of the illicit arts. As we saw in Episode 1.05, Jesse was a faithful journeyman, even rejecting good product because it did not rise to his mentor's uncompromising standards.

High School Teacher

The ineffectual, disrespected, underpaid and under-appreciated high school teacher is a common caricature in modern culture, and it is a largely accurate portrait. Walter White had to be someone ready to break bad; making him an underpaid high school chemistry teacher working a second job was a credible way of achieving this storytelling goal.

Teaching does not have to carry the negative connotations we have chosen to assign to it in our culture. My experience of teaching was very different from Walter White's, even though I taught at precisely the same grade level, following an almost identical syllabus, to teens the same age as those in Walter's class. The difference was culture. Whenever I entered the classroom the students stood at attention and addressed me not even by my surname, but only as "Sir" (actually "Monsieur," since we were in a French-speaking country). If any of my students were in town sitting with friends when I walked by, they would stand and face me out of respect for my position as a "professeur des sciences physiques." Those of my colleagues who were native West Africans were shown perhaps even greater respect, since their students knew that these women and men had overcome extreme adversity to become professeurs. But regardless of our ethnicity or origin, we were respected, even revered, because of our decision to apply our technical expertise to the teaching of children.

There is no longer any such reverence of teachers in Western cultures. We need to keep this cultural fact in mind as we explore Walter's life and decisions. We should also factor in the sad fact that he was obliged to take a second job just to make ends meet, and that his health insurance was inadequate to the financial challenge of providing suitable cancer treatment. Breaking Bad is calling our attention to the deplorable, truly inexcusable fact that healthcare in the United States is sub-par, far lower than the quality one can expect in any other developed country in the world. Upholding the virtue of capitalism in the realm of healthcare is arguably the most important factor in the diminished economic capacity of the country.

I leave it to viewer-participants to decide the importance of cultural and socio-economic factors in Walter's proclamation that he is "awake"—that is, that he has made a free decision, unencumbered by any cultural, social, or familial consideration, to break bad. Is he truly free, or is he slave to forces beyond his control?

One factor we must include in our calculus is the fact that he is a teacher by choice. He could have remained an entrepreneur, but he made a personal decision to withdraw from the company he co-founded. He knew teachers are paid less than scientists in other professions. Though I served as a chemistry and physics teacher in the Peace Corps in Togo, West Africa, when I returned to the United States I didn't even consider a career in teaching. I got into industry as quickly as I could, established myself as a researcher, and worked my way up the technical ladder to the highest scientific rungs. In the last few years I have consistently earned three or four times the salary I would have been paid as an experienced teacher. Walter understood the disparity in compensation as well as I do, but he chose to teach.

Chemistry as Metaphor

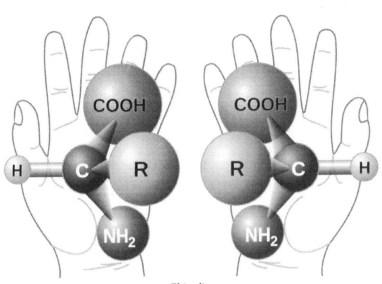

Chirality
National Aeronautics and Space Administration, 2011

"Respect the chemistry." Chemistry is more than a technical discipline. When Walter utters those three words, in Season Three, he is instructing us. But since we know 'chemistry' refers to something greater than subject matter in a lecture hall, we know we are being told to respect something of far greater importance. I have a sense of this greater entity after taking in four and a half seasons of the series, but it is my own personal impression. At this early point in the series—only five or six episodes in—I don't want to paint a full picture. Instead, I want to invite you to look around on your own. When chemistry is invoked as a focal point in an episode, what is really being said?

For instance, in Episode 1.02, Walter explains the idea of chirality. It's a bit advanced for the second day of 11th grade chemistry, but Walter has simplified quite a bit.

Chiral—from the Greek word *hand* [χέρι]. Now the concept here being that just as your left hand and your right hand are mirror images of one another ... identical and yet opposite—well, so too, organic compounds can exist as mirror image forms of one another all the way down to the molecular level.

Although they may look the same, they don't always behave the same. For instance, thalidomide. The right-handed isomer of the drug thalidomide is a perfectly fine,

70

good medicine to give to a pregnant woman to prevent morning sickness. But make the mistake of giving that same pregnant woman the left-handed isomer … and her child will be born with horrible birth defects.

Mirror images. Active, inactive. Good, bad.

Pursuing chemistry as metaphor, we know the stereoisomers under discussion here are not thalidomide, but the far more dangerous substance known as Walter White—who before the end of Season One will be known as the truly lethal entity, Heisenberg.

But what does 'chirality' mean in reference to Walter? Is he one isomer or the other, or a dangerous, misleading mixture of both the right-handed (good, moral) and left-handed (bad or 'sinister,' immoral) stereoisomers? In breaking bad, has he turned from some right-handed, good side of his nature toward a pre-existing left-handed side of his personality, or did he create the Heisenberg persona from whole cloth, entirely from scratch? Did 'chirality' predestine him to criminality? Does 'chirality' mean that he has a *choice* of right-handed responsibility and left-handed criminality? Does 'chirality' mean he needed to consciously activate (decide "I am awake") the bad side of his nature?

I believe Breaking Bad offers us a few responses to the question. We have several examples, after all, and not just Walter White. We are already acquainted with Jesse's drug trafficking, Marie Schrader's kleptomania (1.03) and Hank Schrader's predilection for illicit Cuban cigars (1.07). Soon enough we will learn of Skyler's sins. But we will also have to include important extenuating factors into our analysis; by the end of Season Two many of us may wish to adjust our definitions of 'chirality.'

One of the most important factors we must consider is the effect of family. Over the first four seasons of Breaking Bad we are going to become familiar with not fewer than four families, some of them extending into three or four generations. As we will see, every bond of husband to wife, mother to son, sister to sister, has greater bearing on individual actions than even a desire to remain chirally pure (or enantiomerically contaminated!). Walter needs to tell us to "respect the chemistry," but we require no such instruction regarding our families. A father will sacrifice anything, or commit any deed, for daughter or son. We will look at family bonds in the next chapter.

The White Family Residence
Copyright 2011 Martin Woutisseth, used with permission

Devoted Family Man

"La familia es todo." Hector Salamanca ("Tio") says this in Episode 3.07, but the rule applies equally well throughout Breaking Bad. Family is everything, and nothing anyone does can change that rule. As we will see in coming seasons, the law is so unbending that even greatest necessity cannot dislodge this fundamental principle from its position at the pinnacle of every character's list of priorities. We will see good guys perform unthinkable deeds in the name of family, and we will see bad guys heroically sacrifice all for sons and daughters. Family is the great equalizer, the one value that trumps ethics, morality, good grooming, and causes the most selfish person to surrender everything without a moment's hesitation.

The absolute, inviolate nature of this truth will be pounded into our conscious awareness in powerful, dramatic ways over the next four seasons. The rule will certainly become a major touchstone and more than likely a dramatic turning point near the end of Season Five. The most complete understanding of Breaking Bad philosophy, then, requires that we become well acquainted with the full significance of family to the show's fictional world.

Literary Periodicity

Breaking White ends with the chapter titled He, for Heisenberg. Probably you have figured out that each season of Breaking Bad corresponds to a period in the periodic table of the elements in my full-series companion book, *Breaking Blue*. So,

Season One is given Period One, spanning hydrogen to helium, Season Two is given Period Two, from lithium to neon, and so on. Some of you have already started looking for a chemical element with the symbol 'D' and have come up empty-handed. "I thought this guy was a chemist. Doesn't he know there's no element with atomic symbol D?" Well, yes, I am a chemist, and depending on the chemist you consult with there either is or isn't a chemical element designated by the symbol 'D.' In strictly formal terms there is no element called 'D,' but many chemists apply the symbol D to a common isotope of hydrogen, called deuterium. Deuterium is nothing more than elemental hydrogen with a neutron in the nucleus (ordinary hydrogen has no neutrons—it is the only chemical element bearing this structural distinction). Even those who are not trained in physics or chemistry will have heard of the substance called "heavy water." Heavy water is D_2O, deuterium oxide, composed of two atoms of deuterium ("heavy hydrogen," if you will) and one atom of oxygen.

By considering the periodic table in a way foreign even to some chemists, I am symbolically stating that we need to look at Breaking Bad in more than traditional, tried and true ways. We may even need to move beyond our ordinary comfort zones if we truly wish to enrich our understanding of the series.

It is certainly true that many facets of Breaking Bad characters must be studied if we have any hope of making sense of Walter White's descent into criminality. It is not enough to say that Walter is driven by pride, or that every one of his shortcomings and failures derives of a materialist mindset. This may be true for the cardboard characters offered up in procedural television and shoot-'em-up movies, but any such interpretation of character motivation in Breaking Bad will fall far short of the truth. You cannot watch the first two episodes of Breaking Bad and then skip to Episode 5.08 and seriously believe that you will absorb a complete, balanced and well-informed appreciation of everything that takes place.

You can do this very easily in police procedurals. Watch *Law and Order*, Episode 1.03, then advance to Episode 12.22. Do you have any difficulty understanding any part of the episode twelve *years* into the series? Didn't think so. In fact, you could speak with a fan of the show who had watched every episode from the first 12 seasons. She could confirm that you picked up on all of the important developments in the episode.

Breaking Bad is a serial drama but certain themes, such as family, come up at regular intervals. Attaching my discussion of the show to the periodic table of the elements makes a great deal of sense, symbolically, because I will return to the same or similar topics throughout my analysis of later seasons. Heisenberg, in particular, is assigned an important position at the far-right group in the table, called the Noble Gases. I will explain some of the symbolic significance of this in Chapter He.

A Father's Heart

> My name's Walter Hartwell White. I live at 308 Negra Arroyo Lane, Albuquerque, New Mexico. To all law enforcement authorities, this is not an admission of guilt. I am speaking to my family now. Skyler, you are the love of my life, I hope you know that. Walter Jr., you're my big man. There are ... there are going to be some things ... things that you'll come to learn about me in the next few days. I just want you to know that no ... no matter how it may look, I only had you in my heart. Good-bye.

"There are going to be some things..."—like a dead body, tens of thousands of dollars in cash, and a complete roving methamphetamine laboratory set up in an RV. Oh, and your father was arrested in his underwear forty miles out in the desert. Some things.

Perhaps even then, in the very first minute of Breaking Bad, Walter could not have expected his family's forgiveness or even their understanding, but he could probably count on their love. Early in the series Walter Jr. decides that he has his own identity and he begins to go by the name of Flynn. But as soon as it becomes apparent that Skyler is disrespecting his father, Flynn reverts to Walter Jr. Regardless of anything Walter may have done, his son loves him and will stand by him. Even late in the series we witness acts by Walter, Skyler, and Walter Jr. that could only be attributed to familial love.

Tabula Rasa

Most television and movie heroes are single, divorced, or widowed. If a husband or wife is present, he or she is more often than not entirely absent whenever dramatic actions take place. Captain Kirk roamed the galaxy unattached except for the obligatory single-episode fling with an old flame. President Bartlet was married, it's true, but we never saw Abby in the situation room. When Flight 815 crashed in 2004 there were 72 survivors (I'm counting Vincent), but only two married couples among them.

Perhaps the married couples were preferentially killed on impact? Or maybe married people hardly ever fly together?

Light and Dark
Copyright 2011 Pearson Moore

Having written scenes involving married couples, I think I understand why we rarely see television dramas involving married protagonists: Marriage makes for difficult writing. It's much easier to have a head-strong protagonist with a single agenda than to take the time to write in all the complications associated with married life. An unattached hero can come and go as she pleases without ever having to talk with hubby or find a broom closet big enough to store the kids while she goes out to save the city (or the country, or the galaxy).

That is to say, marriage is inconvenient to drama. Drama is governed by rules of economy. Only those characters that contribute to the dramatic action can be included in a scene. If spouse and children do not contribute to the drama, they cannot be present. An interesting corollary to the Rule of Economy is Chekhov's Gun, which states if a gun appears on stage in Act One we need to see it used at some critical point later in the play. Breaking Bad has made frequent use of this rule throughout the last five years, although only once with an actual gun.

Tabula Rasa, empty slate, is often used in drama to simplify the situation, essentially to force the main players to concentrate on the problem at hand without facing the distractions of real life. Nothing that happened before the stage is set is allowed to complicate the drama. More often than not this is done at the beginning of the novel, with a contrivance of setting: In a lifeboat after the ship was sunk (*Lifeboat*), locked in a jury room upon conclusion of the trial (*Twelve Angry Men*), in the antechamber to heaven (*Steambath*), or in a deserted location after a plane crash (*The Grey*, *Lost*).

Lost is a special case. Portraying almost exclusively unattached, single individuals, *Lost* began with a plane crash (setting *tabula rasa*) on a deserted island (setting *tabula rasa* II) invisible and inaccessible to the outside world (amplification of setting *tabula rasa* II), compounded by literal *tabula rasa*:

KATE: I want to tell you what I did - why he was after me.
JACK: I don't want to know. It doesn't matter, Kate, who we were - what we did before this, before the crash. It doesn't really... three days ago we all died. We should all be able to start over.
(*Lost*, Episode 1.03, "Tabula Rasa")

If *Lost* had relied on these three *tabula rasa* crutches throughout the first season it is unlikely that the series would have been approved for a second season. Probably it would have been forgotten long ago ("Oh, yeah, *Lost*—wasn't that the *Gilligan's Island* remake? Plane crash instead of getting lost at sea?"). One of the things that Lost began to do immediately was to show the futility of *tabula rasa*. About 30% of the show consisted of detailed flashbacks which demonstrated the inexorable trajectory of destiny in the lives of every major character, and many of the minor characters. The Island had ruled their lives long before the crash of Flight 815 and continued to determine their fate for the remainder of the series. By twisting many storytelling conventions into convoluted pretzels, Lost became the groundbreaking television series of the 21st century to which all other dramas of merit are inevitably compared.

Tabula rasa, then, is an over-simplification, a storytelling fantasy that allows the novelist (or playwright or showrunner) to remove the complicating aspects of reality that are normally thought to interfere with economic storytelling. This fantasy reached its high point, I think, in the 1976 soft-erotic film *Laure* (called *Emmanuelle Forever* in the United States). The movie was a kind of erotic treasure hunt, with the ultimate goal of discovering the Mara Tribe in the Philippines. The Mara practiced an annual ritual in which certain members of the tribe were allowed to forget their past, including past relationships. No more husband or wife or children, no responsibilities—a complete and literal *tabula rasa* that would allow the sexually liberated to live their unattached, hedonistic lives. It was the most logical concluding argument of the sexual revolution.

Family and Responsibility

Peasant Family
Le Nain Brothers, circa 1640

A reasonable extrapolation of memory erasure is self-annihilation. If members of the Mara Tribe can forget all past relationships—all responsibilities—the result may initially appear to be freedom for the individual undergoing erasure of memory, but it would mean lack of care for young children, leading to their abandonment or to their attachment to foster parents. Wholesale severing of relationship and abandoning of responsibility would inevitably lead to social disintegration, chaos, and death. Hedonism presents the tantalizing illusion of freedom, but it is actually the surest form of slavery.

The idea that true freedom begins with responsibility seems to be the hidden thesis underlying Breaking Bad's unusual emphasis on family. Breaking Bad rejects *tabula rasa*, insisting on the realistic portrayal of complicated family relationships, not only within the nuclear unit, but including the further complications of extended family.

We are told in the very first minute of the series that family considerations will weigh heavily on Walter's decisions—in fact, his family is more important to him than just about any other aspect of his life. We know this because rather than hiding or plotting an escape or devising an excuse, Walter's first thought is to provide a video apology to his family. This is a crucial dramatic revelation of Walter's inner self and an indication of the direction of future decision points in the series. Far from pushing family to the periphery, Breaking Bad will insist on bringing Skyler, Junior, and (later) Holly to center stage. Every major character is attached to family and not an artificially independent agent. Even Walter's antagonists have family, and some of them have important extended family, too, whose relationships are detailed onscreen.

In Season One we are introduced to two antagonists: Hank Schrader and Tuco Salamanca. Hank is not only married, but he is wed to Skyler's sister, Marie, making him Walter's brother in law. Tuco Salamanca seems initially to fall into the standard loner bad guy role, but before the end the first season we learn that Tuco also has an important relative, Tio Hector (the old man in the wheelchair). The unusual emphasis on family ought to serve as a clue regarding the significance of Hector Salamanca. He's not just some colorful background to Tuco's antics; Hector will prove critical to events throughout Seasons Two, Three, and Four.

Later in the series we will meet an antagonist to Walter who appears to have no familial connections, but for the very reason that he seems disconnected he will immediately raise our suspicions about him. Eventually we will learn of a connection, a man the antagonist insists is family, but the nature of the antagonist's 'family' will only serve to raise even more suspicions about him. But this antagonist, like every other major character, will base his actions first of all on family considerations.

Jesse and Jake

Jesse seems at first to be the outlier in Breaking Bad's story of conflicted families. He has no wife, no children, and not even a girlfriend (unless we count the well-endowed woman who throws his clothes out the second-story window in the pilot episode).

I am going to say something here that may well be at odds with the opinion of most viewers of the complete five-season series: *Jesse's family connections are deeper and more important than those of any other character in the series*. I can build a logical case for this assertion, but my position probably ought to be considered to occupy the realm of opinion rather than carrying any objective validity. The argument I intend to make throughout Breaking Blue will depend on this statement.

Many important events involving Walter's sidekick in later seasons will alter viewer-participant evaluation of Jesse's significance to the story. However, since my original impression of Jesse and Jake has remained unperturbed since Season One, I do not feel any scruples in relaying my opinion about him early in the first period of our 'periodic' examination of the series.

Jake seems to be everything that Jesse is not. An academic achiever of unusual distinction, Jacob Pinkman has received awards and honors not only in his extracurricular coursework ("Most Distinguished Mathlete"), but also in sports and in citizenship ("Environmental Consciousness Award"). As if that were not enough, he plays the piccolo and has full command of the English language.

But it turns out that Jacob and Jesse are alike in two important ways. The marijuana cigarette that Jesse's parents consider the final straw is not Jesse's but Jake's. Ironically, the joint becomes Adam Pinkman's rationale for kicking Jesse out of their house. Jesse and Jacob share an interest in illicit drugs, and this fact causes Jesse an additional degree of discomfort after being evicted.

Jake: Thanks for not telling on me. Think I could have it back?
Jesse: [Grinding the pot into the sidewalk under his shoe] It's skunk weed anyway.

The most obvious conclusion we might draw from this interaction is that Jesse disapproves of his younger brother's forays into "gateway drugs." Or perhaps he's upset that Jacob's experimentation with pot is the unjust cause of his eviction. Or, less likely but still consistent with the scenario, Jesse thinks "skunk weed" is beneath the dignity of his accomplished and talented brother.

I want to offer an opinion for your consideration. We could argue that Jesse is upset with his parents because they are kicking him out, and angry with Jake for the essentially unrelated reason that his younger brother is experimenting with drugs. That is, we might come away from this scene believing that many things are on Jesse's mind, that several facts related to his family are causing discomfort in his personal life.

I believe a reasonable and possibly stronger alternative take-home idea is that Jesse is experiencing a single source of pain in the scenes involving his brother, and that that pain is the same in the first scene as in the final one: Jesse is sad that he and his brother are both estranged from their parents.

Pay close attention to the scene in Jake's room in Episode 1.04. Jake is absorbed in homework on his computer rather than engaging with his older brother. But there is an element of this scene that will immediately raise the concerns of every parent taking in the proceedings: Jake is on the computer, in his room, and *the door is closed.* Responsible parents—parents who engage with their children—do not allow young children to access the Internet without constant supervision. I am not commenting on Adam Pinkman's parenting skills. Rather, I am simply pointing out that the closed bedroom door and the computer in a child's room could be considered signs of unnecessary distance between parents and son.

The only portrait we have of Jacob Pinkman is that of a child withdrawn, disengaged, essentially on his own and alienated—estranged—from his parents.

Two Boys in a Landscape
(A young boy and his protective older brother)
Herman Mijnert Donker, circa 1652

I believe it is this mode of alienated existence that is the second way in which Jesse and Jake are alike. Jesse is old enough to feel pain for his younger brother, pain for Jake's distance from their parents. Pain, because he knows Jake is ignorant of the damage his estrangement from his parents will wreak in his young life. I believe the greatest pain in Jesse's life is his alienation from his mother and father. If we look at the Pinkman home scenes in this way, in which Jesse's pain is the result of familial alienation, the dynamic becomes simple, easy to understand, but more important to our comprehension of the greater series, this view is consistent with the thesis of family's centrality to Breaking Bad's message.

Skyler and Walter

Regardless of the placement of alienation in the prioritization table of Breaking Bad themes, we must consider the role of Walter's secret life and its effect on those closest to him. Walter tells us in his Scene One confession that family is paramount to him, and the first member of his family he mentions on the video is his wife, Skyler.

I believe it is essential to keep in mind that Walter's emotional withdrawal from Skyler did not begin with his illicit drug activity. It didn't even begin with his diagnosis of lung cancer. In fact, we are led to believe that emotional distance has been a feature of their marriage, on both sides, for many years.

After Walter has been humiliated by Skyler and Hank—and at his 50th birthday party, no less—Skyler gives him a late-night birthday present in bed: a hand job while she focuses on her eBay transactions. While she stares at the screen and masturbates him with one hand under the covers, they discuss such romantic and erotic topics as the car wash, driving to Los Alamos to see the Mars rover photographs, and painting the house. Just as Walter seems to respond to her half-hearted, essentially peripheral ministrations, Skyler's eyes grow big and she seems excited. "Yes! Fifty-six!" she shouts. Her excitement has nothing to do with Walter; the cause of her joyous … ah … ejaculation (sorry, I couldn't resist) is not Walter's physical state, but her unexpected victory on eBay. Her small revenue-generating initiatives mean more to her than a few brief moments of intimacy with her husband. In fact, the scene indicates her emotions are devoid of any sense of intimacy.

The series of scenes in which Walter learns of his cancer and short moments later divulges not the slightest hint of health problems to Skyler is confirmation that neither of them is in a position of emotional intimacy or even emotional honesty with each other.

All of this happens prior to Walter's decision to break bad. Walter's transition from Walter Bland to Walter Mitty (his dreams of wealth when he sees Hank's drug bust on television) to Heisenberg is facilitated by the fact that he has not been emotionally or factually accountable to his wife or to anyone else for a long, long time.

We should acknowledge two possible, perhaps likely, consequences of his emotional detachment from Skyler.

First, Walter has been existing in an emotional desert for a long and unhealthy period time. It is difficult to image even a strong individual being able to exist indefinitely under such conditions without actively seeking some positive change.

Second, as we continue to witness events that may be considered triggers for Walter's decision to break bad, commit murder, or perform other criminal deeds, I think we need to keep in mind the chronological precedence of Walter's emotional distance from Skyler. It is entirely possible that later events could be the result of factors other than Walter's lack of emotional connection. Recall the "chemistry" between Walter and Gretchen in Episode 1.03, for example. We are led to believe that at least for a time Walter enjoyed an emotionally close relationship with Gretchen, but at the same time he held views that did not include the possibility of a spiritual dimension to human life. Thus, his emotional withdrawal later in life, with Skyler, may be the major factor in his turn to illicit drugs, or it may be only one of several decisive influences. Yet another possibility is that the emotional distance evident in Episode 1.01 is itself the result of some earlier occurrence or state of being. I will discuss trigger conditions and events at greater length in Chapter T.

Walter and Jesse

Admiral McCain and Commander McCain
Vice Admiral John S. McCain, Sr., with his son, Cmdr. John S. McCain, Jr.
U.S. Navy, 2 September 1945

Walter White and Jesse Pinkman have a strained relationship but we know Jesse is the protégé to **Mr. White**, the exalted mentor. Jesse will continue to address Walter as Mr. White throughout the five seasons, even as they experience the majority of the show's most frightening and game-changing events side by side. Walter will never be Jesse's equal, but always his superior.

We might expect just such an asymmetrical relationship, strictly on the basis of the age differential or the stunning disparity in technical expertise. But theirs is not a loose or distant student-teacher affiliation. Due to the fact that they cannot discuss the nature of their illicit activities with anyone else, they will naturally develop the intimate kind of rapport associated with only the closest of mentor-protégé relationships. It seems reasonable that any such close proximity and the sharing of information only between themselves could lead to something more like a liaison or a family bond.

In light of Breaking Bad's strong emphasis on the importance of family, the slow evolution of a father-son relationship—perhaps even an emotional bond—between Walter and Jesses seems possible or even likely. I imagine Walter's emotional distance from his wife and son and Jesse's (possible) feeling of alienation from his father may tend to enhance the potential for an emotional, family-like bond between the two men.

The importance of these possibilities, in my mind, is not so much the proliferation of quasi-familial relations between people not related by blood, but rather the establishment of a kind of conceptual topography or matrix of different ways of thinking about family, friendship, relationship, responsibility, and the inter-related topics and themes that flow directly from those ideas.

If it is true that family relationships are the basis of emotional or spiritual freedom in the Breaking Bad universe, could Walter become Jesse's spiritual salvation, or vice versa? Could Jesse supply Walter with emotional riches sufficient to propel him out of whatever psychological malfunction or deficit of the soul that allowed him to actively pursue a life of crime? If family is the source of true happiness in Breaking Bad, could it be that family is the only means of true conversion?

We have been led to believe that all of these considerations will become moot in the case of Walter. Mr. Chips must become Scarface, after all. Perhaps an endgame conversion of the soul is possible for Walter, but even if it is not, possibly other players in the saga will benefit from the influence or intervention of family or friend. As we will see in coming seasons, Walter is not the only character who will wade neck-deep into the chemical sewer he has built. Characters we now consider innocent will succumb to raw temptation, while others who seem beyond redemption will begin to show signs of potential healing and growth.

Regardless of the details, we can be sure of one constant in the world of Breaking Bad: La familia es todo. It is as constant and regular as the periodic (repeating) motion of a pendulum—or the periodic resurfacing of themes in every season of a most fascinating television program.

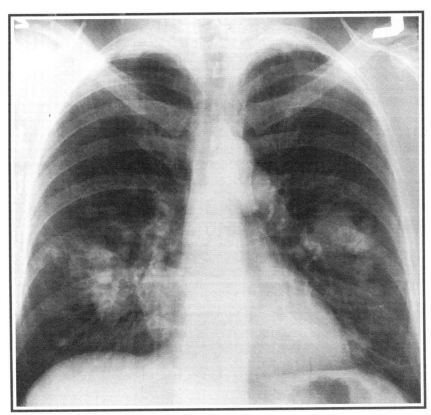

X-Ray Evidence of Advanced Lung Cancer
National Cancer Institute 2009

Chapter T

Trigger Conditions & Events

Tritium is an unstable isotope of hydrogen. It has a short half-life, and it decays not into hydrogen, but into helium, an element with properties very different from those it started with. Hydrogen is always ready to form bonds with other elements. Hydrogen, for example, burns in the presence of oxygen to form water. Helium, though, is a loner. It never combines with oxygen, or any other element for that matter.

From our anthropomorphic point of view for the purposes of this book, we could say helium is too proud to create bonds with other elements. In our 'periodic' scheme in this book, Hydrogen refers to high school teacher Walter White, while Helium refers to the proud loner, Heisenberg. Continuing our chemistry analogy, Tritium is the state Walter occupies at the critical decision point between Walter White, chemistry teacher, and Heisenberg, notorious drug lord. Our study of tritium focuses on the trigger conditions and events that lead Walter to the knife-edge decision between the ordinary life of teacher and devoted father, and the extraordinary life of a criminal übermensch.

Pre-Existing Condition

We learned in the first breakfast scene of Walter's pre-existing condition. Not lung cancer or shortness of breath. Not fainting spells or cough. Walter's pre-existing condition was lack of manliness. He allowed his wife and son and everyone else to walk all over him. Rather than bringing home the bacon, he ended up working a second job, only to be given the task of cleaning and shining the sports car belonging to the same student who had insulted and disrespected him in chemistry class. "Oh my God," the boy's girlfriend squealed into her mobile phone, "you would not believe who's cleaning Ted's car!"

Weight Gain Advertisement
Unknown artist, circa 1920

Walter escaped the degrading insults at the car wash only to experience them heaped up and flowing over in his own home at his surprise birthday party.

"Glock 22," Hank says, pulling out his quite substantial sidearm. "That's my daily carry.... You forget the 9-mil, alright. I've seen one of those bounce off a windshield one time. When you gotta bring a gun, baby, you gotta bring enough gun. Forty cal."

When Hank hands the unloaded gun to Junior, Walt, in his feeble voice, tries to note his disapproval, but Junior and Hank are so absorbed they don't pay attention to the emasculated entity whose birthday party they're celebrating.

Junior hands Walter the weapon but he doesn't even want to touch it. He finally takes it and seems surprised.

Walter:[Hefting the Glock] It's just heavy.
Hank: That's why they hire men! [Motioning to Walter, grinning] Hey, it's not gonna bite you, alright. [Turning to his DEA friends] Looks like Keith Richards with a glass of warm milk, eh?
[DEA guys laugh]

When Hank offers a toast the only positive compliment he can think of is that Walter's "heart is in the right place." Then he grabs Walter's beer and shouts "Na zdrowi!" [Polish: To your health] Before Walter can say anything, Hank blurts out, "Hey, turn to Channel Three!" For the next three minutes we see Hank Schrader, local DEA hero, being interviewed on KCAV television regarding his latest meth lab bust.

It is Walter's party, but he has to endure disgrace piled on top of contempt, everyone laughs at him, and he isn't allowed to toast his own health. In a final insult, Hank steals away any attention Walter may have had and focuses everyone on himself, the man's man who carries a real weapon and busts bad guys and drug dealers.

What occurs next is telling. Walter is off by himself, far away from the television, until the news reporter begins to talk about the money Hank seized. The video shows what must be hundreds of thousands of dollars in thick, tight rolls. Walter walks toward the group and stares at the screen.

Walter:Hank, how much money is that?
Hank: Ah, it's about 700 grand. Pretty good haul.
Walter:Wow. That's unusual isn't it, that kind of cash?
Hank: It's not the most we ever took. It's easy money—'til we catch you!

Walter is all but drooling in response to the sight on the television screen. This is probably not the typical response of a citizen viewing video of a drug seizure; no one else gathered around the television appears to share Walter's fascination with the visuals. The important aspect of this scene to me, as I attempt to identify a rationale for Walter's later decisions, is that the celebration of Hank's success, and the revelation of Walter's lust for easy money, occurs a full day before Walter learns of his medical condition.

Resignation or Resolve

Thumbs Up
Pfc. Shawn Williams, seriously injured by an IED, gives the Thumbs Up sign
Kandahar Province, Afghanistan
Lt. J. G. Haraz Ghanbari, U.S. Navy, 17 June 2011, PD

I hope no one reading this book ever has to hear the words Walter's doctor directed at him: that he had inoperable Stage Three lung cancer and he was not likely to live. I am among those who has had to sit on Walter's side of the desk to hear a prognosis no one should ever have to confront.

In late 1995 my wife was diagnosed with Stage IIIA breast cancer. The prognosis was only marginally better than Walter White's: The oncology team gave my wife a 50% chance of living another five years.

Fight or flight? Confront the cancer head-on and beat it, or run away and wait for death to come?

I suppose there are people who crumble, who decide to throw in the towel at the first mention of a terminal diagnosis. I don't suppose my wife and I are alone, though, in the kind of reaction we had. We made arrangements for treatment, for babysitters so I could continue working. We researched doctors, treatment plans, advanced surgeries, innovative imaging options. I cooked the meals, washed the dishes, took care of the kids, did the laundry, did the shopping, took care of my wife, talked with her doctors and surgeons and technicians every day, drover her to and from treatments and surgeries, *and* worked 40 hours every week. A schedule, I suppose, that most working women are used to.

The bottom line is that neither Kim nor I ever thought of giving up, even when the X-rays, MRIs, and sonograms were discouraging at best, even when treatments showed no sign of reducing the cancer. We just kept on fighting, working hard, keeping our spirits up. Even when things looked their worst, we smiled, kept our chins high, gave the thumbs up. This didn't go on for days or weeks. We didn't have to keep up this extraordinary effort and mind-numbing, wearying discipline for months. We did it for two and a half *years*. We never crumbled. We never stopped.

As Jonathan Quincy Taggart would say, Never give up, never surrender.

Why did Walter cave? Why did he initially choose not to fight?

The situation my wife and I faced was different from Walter's in two important respects. First, my medical insurance back in 1995 would cover most of the tests and treatment, and second, the times and my verbal skills were such that I was willing—eager—to fight for every test and round of treatment my wife would need.

But times, as they say, have changed. By any account, healthcare in the United States is no longer what it was in 1995. Health insurance costs more and delivers less than in any other developed country in the world.

Poverty and Death or Bankruptcy and Death

In 2004 the popular Canadian television host and commentator George Stroumboulopoulos ("Strombo") took on the task of advocating for his hero, Tommy Douglas, to be chosen as the Greatest Canadian. Tommy Douglas could claim dozens of important social and cultural advances during a career that spanned over fifty years, not just for his home province of Saskatchewan, but for all of Canada. Tommy is the Father of Canadian Medicare. If you get sick in Canada, the last thing you have to worry about is how you're going to pay. It's taken care of for you. It's called universal healthcare.

Strombo would probably agree that of the ten advocates, he had the easiest case to make. But excellent showman that he is, Strombo didn't take any chances. He chose as his visual one of the small concrete boundary markers defining the border between the United States and Canada, and there he made his final pitch.

91

George Stroumboulopoulos

This is what it all boils down to: The 49th parallel. It's the dividing line between our way, and their way. And did you know, that on that side [pointing to the United States] every thirty seconds someone declares bankruptcy because of medical bills. What I'm saying is Americans go broke—being sick. And I just can't tell you how glad I am we don't live that way. That's all thanks to Tommy.

In Tommy Douglas' words:

I think that medical care is so important that it ought not have a price tag on it. I think that we have come to the place where medical care, like education, ought to be available to every citizen, irrespective of their financial state.

Tommy Douglas won the competition. For the last eight years he has been known as "The Greatest Canadian," and it's because he created Canadian universal healthcare that he is honored with a title no one else can claim.

The Honourable Tommy Douglas
Copyright 1971 The Mighty Quill, CC-SA 3.0

In most countries, the choices Walter faced would include a shorter, more aggressive treatment, or less aggressive treatment aimed at allowing him to continue working while therapies continued. Death would not be an option. In the United States, unless he could call upon almost limitless reserves of cash, his choices were abject poverty followed by death, or bankruptcy followed by death.

My wife lived past the five year mark. In fact, she is in better health than most women her age. Almost every day she says she is thankful that cancer struck 17 years ago and not now. If either of us were to receive today a diagnosis similar to the one Kim heard in the mid-1990s, our paltry health insurance would ensure our death, regardless of our willingness or eagerness to fight.

Why did Walter cave?

Surely we have to consider his psychological state, but I think we can also look to his training as a scientist and his logical, realistic outlook. Given the less than adequate coverage provided by his health insurance, he must have known that fighting the cancer was futile. Even if he sold everything he owned, at some point early in treatment he would have exhausted his financial resources, and treatments would come to an end. He would die, regardless of any amount of fighting he did—Grabthar's Hammer or not.

Social and Personal Accountability

There is no single rationale for Walter's decision to break bad. We could place some degree of blame for Walter's financial predicament on the barbaric socio-economic system of the United

States. The self-destructive tax structure favoring the wealthy, the glaring lack of adequate healthcare for U.S. citizens, and regressive, neo-feudal social structures are destroying what was once a great country. To believe that the monstrous conditions of the United States, in which children and the poor are simply allowed to die, are blameless in this matter constitutes a strong element of fantasy thinking.

"The Mad Scientist"
Bela Lugosi as the Mad Scientist in *The Devil Bat*
Unknown photographer, Producers Releasing Corp., 1940, PD

For the sake of clarity let us go to an extreme view of the situation. Let us posit that the U.S. healthcare system is barbaric. Let us agree that a system that rewards powerful plutocrats who siphon off money for corporate and personal gain rather than allowing for adequate medical treatment would be considered not only less than civilized, but actually criminal and sinful in any other developed culture.

Even if we grant all of this, though, we are left with the fact that Walter decided to manufacture methamphetamine to earn enough money to leave his family a nest egg after his death. This question, I believe, must be considered apart from any condition of social depravity.

I am well compensated in my position as Principal Scientist to a thriving pharmaceutical company. I have enjoyed several decades of financial ease. Even so, there have been times, especially early in my life, when I had barely the resources to feed and house myself. I have suffered prolonged periods in which I was one paycheck away from homelessness. But I enjoyed then the same unusual, highly specialized knowledge and skillset that has made me useful to companies throughout North America. In particular, I certainly have Walter White's level of expertise, and in exactly those areas that would make it easy for me to manufacture the highest quality methamphetamine. In addition, I have rare skills given short shrift in Breaking Bad. Isolate ricin from *Ricinus communis*? It's not all that difficult.

My deepest expertise is in crystallization, but the area of expertise in which I am most useful is the extraction and purification of high-value chemicals from biological matrices—from plants, animals, fermentation broths, and marine sources. I could, if I were so inclined, help companies isolate botulinum neurotoxins or even more deadly toxins. I could lead efforts to weaponize the material. But I don't. I could sell my expertise to companies of questionable repute. But I don't.

There have been opportunities. There are always opportunities. One of the most interesting of these involved the isolation of a particularly high-value material from soybeans in the early 1990s. The work was highly confidential. Out of the blue one day I received an invitation to interview with one of the world's largest private companies. I was not looking for a job at the time, my name was not in circulation. Somehow this company's agents had found me, but it went much deeper than that. I refused to miss a day of work. Fine, fine, they said, we'll interview you on Saturday. They flew me across the continent on a Friday red-eye to their world headquarters, gave me a very nice hotel suite. On Saturday I found the interview consisted of a brief tour of the world class facilities (very impressive!)—with emphasis on a lab devoted to soybean studies. And then I was asked to give my presentation. I handed the company's Executive Vice President a list of five topics I would not discuss, four of which were bogus subjects, the fifth was the soybean research. I began my presentation, but I was interrupted less than fifteen minutes into it. "Tell us about your soybean work," the Director of R&D said. I politely declined. The questions persisted, and it became clear from the gist of their very forceful inquiries that they knew exactly what I was working on. All they wanted to know was how I was doing it, and how I was able to do it at a much lower cost than they could. I declined to respond to their questions. During their impolite, unethical barrage I finally sat down. "I'm done with my presentation," I told them. I thanked them for their time, gathered my things, and called a taxi. I stomped the vile dust off my feet before getting into the taxi.

It was the most egregious instance of attempted industrial espionage I witnessed in my career. The criminals with whom I had shared a conference room represented a company that every few years is found guilty of price rigging or other illegal behavior. They are routinely slapped with fines in the hundreds of millions of dollars which they pay with essentially zero effect on their bottom line. It was clear to me, sitting in the toxic, ethically noxious environment of that research building, that these individuals were used to getting what they wanted, regardless of the damage they caused to other companies.

The point of this story is not to paint me as some kind of paragon of morality. The fact is, most of you reading these words would behave in precisely the same manner, given the temptations that Walter or I have faced in our professional careers. The greater point I wish to make is that any of us, put into a situation in which we are given the opportunity to make fantastic amounts of money through illicit channels, will instead choose to do what is right, even if this means unusual suffering for ourselves and our families. We would do this regardless of the social accountability weighed against our civilization for any of its moral shortcomings.

Wouldn't Walter behave in the same manner? Even though the enormous piles of cash he saw in the video record of Hank's meth bust were attractive, wouldn't he have chosen the high road rather than descending to ethical depravity for the sake of personal gain?

Given a broad range of circumstances we could consider adequate to social health, I don't believe there's any question: Walter would have done the right thing. The problem is that the circumstances Walter inhabited failed to coincide with normalcy. Something about his experience drove him to consider the production of addictive poison simply to realize a financial windfall. I don't think there can be any question regarding the role of his cancer prognosis as the singular and final trigger event. I am concerned with the trigger conditions, the factors that so warped his mental state that he was able to succumb to animal lusts.

Strength and Weakness

In painting our portrait of the pre-Heisenberg Walter White we will become misled if we do not include the bold and vivid strokes that capture his unusual brilliance. Walter White, at one time in his career, had the potential to achieve limitless wealth, power, and influence. He could have been on the cover of *Scientific American* or *Time*, right next to Elliott Schwartz. We know he harbors the same extraordinary abilities he proved in his creation of Gray Matter Technologies—his skillset has neither deteriorated nor become obsolete, as we learned at Elliott's party. Even now, decades after his seminal contributions to crystallography and positron emission spectrometry, he could easily and quickly become an influential leader in imaging technology, solid state chemistry, or any number of cutting edge disciplines. Instead, he has chosen to withdraw, to hide his talents under a basket.

Samson and Delilah
Max Liebermann 1902

It is because of this dramatic choice, among other facts of Walter White's background, that I believe we are being asked to consider Walter's decision to break bad as entirely his own, as a meditation on personal rather than social forces. Walter White is not a victim of the times, a victim of circumstance, a victim of anything. Breaking Bad is not social commentary, but morality play. Blame society if you will for Walter's unfair financial burden. Blame fate for giving him cancer. Blame Gretchen and Skyler for their inability or unwillingness to engage sexually and intimately. But in the end, I feel, we must limit accountability for the decision to break bad to Walter alone.

Near the end of Skyler's "intervention" we learn an essential facet of Walter's mindset.

Walter: What I want—what I need—is a choice.
Skyler: What does that mean?

Walter:Sometimes I feel like I never actually make any of my own choices, I mean. My entire life—it just seems like I never had a say—about any of it.

He knows he is no ordinary man. He is a Samson of the laboratory, a rare, clear-thinking researcher who can push beyond the shortsightedness of current science, a gifted thinker with the kind of intellectual resources and innate curiosity that drive discovery and creation of technological benefits for all humankind. He knows this because he knows his brainchild, Gray Matter, is thriving and delivering what had only been a dream and a promise back in the early years.

In his mind, though, he is the victim. He is Samson shorn of hair, reduced to intellectual infirmity by the forces arrayed against him. "I never actually make any of my own choices," he said, and the fundamental choice forced upon him was Gray Matter. Gretchen was his Delilah, probing him for weakness, finding it, and forcing him to choose, backing him into a corner so only a single course of action remained. Poor unappreciated, unloved, unrecognized Walter.

Gray, of course, is metaphor. Gray is collaboration, give and take, sharing. It is the concept of contributing to an entity greater than self, greater than White or Black (or Schwartz). It is the willingness to give of oneself, to surrender oneself to such an extent that some attractive facet is lost, becomes inextricably mixed into something else. The purity of White is lost in the collaboration with Schwartz to form Gray. "Molecules: Molecules change their bonds. Elements: They *combine* and change into compounds. Well, that's all of life, right?" Yes, that is pretty much all of life— to give of oneself to form something greater.

We could blame his parents. Or his teachers. Or the neighborhood he grew up in. At some point, though, a man becomes accountable, even if that man was repeatedly a victim in his youth. If he is a human being, if he shares in the necessary qualities we associate with civilized, moral life, he will take a stand against propagating the same injustices that plagued him in years past. Perhaps in some cases this stand requires unusual moral fortitude, but it is society's firm demand nevertheless.

I wonder if Walter ever broke bad. I wonder if his constitution was such that he was not only receptive to the assertion of his tighty-whitey pride, but that the way his brain was wired, the way his soul was configured, somehow determined that he would never combine with anyone to "change into compounds," that he would never surrender any part of himself to create a more enduring, more meaningful entity.   Maybe Walter White was always Heisenberg.

Heisenberg
Copyright 2011 Martin Woutisseth
Used with permission

Chapter He

He²isenberg

A Google search for Heisenberg + "Breaking Bad" returns seven hundred thousand web pages. Tens of thousands of artists have painted, drawn, sculpted, and otherwise rendered Heisenberg's image in hundreds of media types, from oil paints and watercolors on canvas to ink pen on Styrofoam, from papier-mâché to bronze, and every conceivable medium in between. Heisenberg is one of television's most fascinating fictional creations, ranking with Mr. Spock (*Star Trek*), Kramer (*Seinfeld*), Locke (*Lost*), and J. R. Ewing (*Dallas*).

Heisenberg's appeal must be due in large measure to the unusual, expressive range of Bryan Cranston's face and the stunning costuming choice of dark jacket, dark glasses, and black felt pork pie hat. But the enduring nature of Heisenberg's artistic appeal must derive of his standing as one of television's most memorable anti-heroes. He attracts because he disgusts.

There is more to our attraction than loving him, or loving to hate him. We see in Heisenberg the potential of anyone to break bad. A responsible father, a high school teacher—an ordinary guy—can become the most abhorrent sociopath. Even those who base their actions on solid and pure motivations, those who are in every way "awake," may descend into a way of life that independent observers would label immoral, unethical, or criminal.

But there is much more to Heisenberg. The majority of the next four seasons will become an extended meditation on the full meaning of this character's philosophy of life, motivations, thought patterns and behaviors. He will change in ways we could not have expected, and we will have to adjust and adapt our assumptions about the relation of character traits we assume are common to the human condition. We will be surprised to learn that the connections are different than those we thought we could rely upon.

We begin our discussion with this idea: Cancer did not create Heisenberg. In fact, Heisenberg did not originate with any negative concept, event, or condition. His genesis was in Breaking Bad's most consistently positive theme: Family created Heisenberg.

Call to Manhood

David by Michelangelo, circa 1504
Photograph copyright 2005 Rico Heil, GNU-FDL 1.2

"I am awake."

Walter's diagnosis of terminal cancer gave him a reason to engage. His life to that point had been nothing more than demoralized, painful survival at the uninvolved, uncommitted, disengaged periphery of life. Now he had a reason to live. More important to his fundamental identity, though, he had a mechanism for asserting his manhood.

Skyler, Hank, Marie, and even Walter's own son, had all laughed and poked fun at him, abused and disrespected him, and in general considered him not a true father or husband. Because family is central to Breaking Bad, Walter's inability to provide, to fulfill the minimum expectations of a family, meant that he was not truly a man. Now Walter knew he would die, but he realized he could leave his family an enduring legacy. The money he made through the sale of methamphetamine would keep his family housed, clothed, and fed for years, and would even pay for their unborn baby's college. Whenever his family thought of him, even decades after his death, their first thought would be, "Dad provided. He was the perfect father and husband. He was everything a man should be." Walter's legacy would become the unassailable proof of his manhood. How many men could die in the knowledge that their families would think them extraordinary, noble exemplars of masculine fortitude and self-sacrifice?

Walter in Season One did not express a desire to live. He acquiesced to Skyler's "intervention" and agreed to treatment only because this was her wish, not because he truly wanted to endure the rigors of treatment only to face certain death after such a prolonged period of suffering.

Walter "woke up," became vitally engaged in life, not because he was anxious to please Skyler or hope against hope that he could find some way to survive terminal cancer. He woke up because he wished to leave a legacy. We wanted people to think "I wish I could be a real man, like the great and noble Walter White, who spared nothing and sacrificed all for his family."

I don't want to claim at this early point that I have a full grasp of Walter's true motivations. Even four and a half seasons into Breaking Bad I don't think I can claim to have such clear insight into Walter White's being. I think it is possible that we are not meant to have any such insight. Are we supposed to know how "chirality" applies to Walter White? I believe the concept is something to consider as an ongoing question and not a position upon which we must build a rational, syllogistic argument.

I would like to suggest that we may look at Walter's desire to leave his family a nest egg in at least four ways.

Four Winds of Change

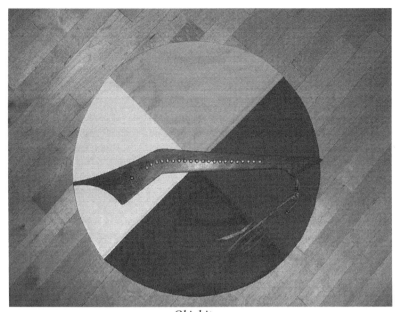

Okichitaw
Four Directions: East, South, North, West
Photograph by Flmgnra, 2008, PD

East Wind: Creativity, Balance, Confidence

First, Walter's move to break bad may have been only the most obvious sign of a radical re-engagement with life, catalyzed by a terminal diagnosis of cancer. In the past he and Skyler had enjoyed no more intimacy than a handjob while she monitored sales on eBay and he talked about painting the house. But now all that would change. Walter's new enthusiasm for life would bring zest to their love life, he would become engrossed in his son's interests, and every day would be approached as a new adventure and yet another opportunity to fully participate in every aspect of his family's life. Maybe for the first time in his life he would enjoy and project the kind of balance and confidence that are the cherished benefits of a life in order.

North Wind: Courage, Energy, Knowledge

Second, Walter's decision to break bad may have been informed by multiple underlying motivations, conditions, and events. Let us recall that Walter seemed to have no firm concept of the spiritual nature of human reality. If Breaking Bad is an examination of motives and desires and ways of thinking, perhaps we ought to consider Walter's materialist outlook as a kind of blinder that prevented him from seeing and following routes to fatherhood and husbandhood. Walter could not be the kind of father and husband others might have liked because he lacked the philosophical, psychological, and emotional resources required in these types of relationships. However, he still wished to be a father and husband, and in leaving a financial legacy to his family he was at least demonstrating his good intentions. Perhaps part of becoming "awake" was a sudden self-awareness, not only of his biological mortality, but also of the limitations of character that impinged on his abilities as father and husband. If he achieved this level of self-awareness it is difficult to imagine this new knowledge would not affect his decisions and actions. Taking positive steps on behalf of his family, in the face of personal limitations, would demonstrate a rare species of courage that would only strengthen his legacy and reputation.

South Wind: Success, Focus, Strength

Third, consider the jockey underwear as a guiding image in our examination of possibilities. Walter was proud. Hank understood Walter's decision to forego cancer treatment as a manifestation of pride, and I believe we are justified in considering his mindset in this light. Maybe Walter White was not only psychologically incapable of choosing to serve his family (due to a materialistic understanding of life or due to any other factor we might like to draw from his backstory) but he was philosophically opposed to the interactions inherent in family life. He was proud, therefore aloof, separate, distinct.

Walter was proud. He could not participate in Gray Matter because Gray (White mixed with Black or Schwartz) meant giving up White, surrendering himself to a greater entity. This surrender of self is the very essence of family life, and especially for parents. Being a father means surrendering, sacrificing self for the good of children and spouse. Because Walter was proud, he could never be a true parent, he would never enjoy real intimacy with his wife. His legacy, on the other hand, was an obtainable goal because it did not require of him any surrender to a family-style Gray Matter enterprise. All he had to do to achieve a positive reputation that would outlive him was to give the appearance of having been a loving, engaged parent. A financial nest egg would provide a tangible proof of his strength as a father, his success as a husband.

West Wind: Choice, Challenge, Proof

Finally, a central principle of Breaking Bad is change. Chemistry—metaphorically our meditation on Walter White—is "the study of change." If we accept change as a primary element of this journey, Walter White will necessarily exist in a different philosophical and psychological state at the beginning than he will at the end of the adventure. It seems likely that anything as important as the factor determining Walter's decision to break bad would be one most subject to change.

But what kinds of change should we be looking for? One way of changing could be an instantaneous break. He was proud in Episode 3.05, but all of a sudden in Episode 3.06 he was humble. A second mode of change would be gradual movement along a continuum. He started from a materialistic point of view, but possibly over the course of several seasons he will gradually become grounded in spiritual understanding and practice. He will move from agnostic high school teacher to church-going gangster.

I think there's another way of looking at this, and it involves the frequent touchstone of chirality. We don't know with any certainty what chirality is supposed to mean, as I have already mentioned in earlier essays. In the same way, we don't know what "change" is supposed to entail in Walter's life, but one of the possible routes of change, it seems to me, is personal volition. Maybe all of the negative and positive character attributes determining Walter's outlook and behavior at the end of the final season were already present at the beginning of the first season. Perhaps change, as we experience it over the course of Breaking Bad, will focus mostly on Walter White's decision to unleash character traits that were earlier suppressed or neglected. Challenges over the next seasons will result in the growing importance of personal choice.

Heisenberg: Family Man

The decision to break bad is not connected to the choice to become Heisenberg.

Consider an angry and determined man who has made a sudden change in life and is now resolved to act against his enemies and pursue his interests. He acquires innovative weapons, confronts those who stand in his way, kills his enemies, and enjoys the spoils of his aggression.

This could be a description of Heisenberg, but it could just as easily be a description of a kind-hearted man whose company we appreciate, whose presence in the neighborhood is not only positive, but reassuring to everyone. The man we speak of is a federal law enforcement agent, and we are glad to hear that when he confronts armed criminals he is firm, stands his ground, and if they do not yield, he disarms or even kills them. Those who oppose Hank Schrader in the meth labs see him as an angry, ominous, unyielding presence. Rightfully so, and bully for Hank.

Migrant Father with His Young Son
Unknown photographer, Environmental Protection Agency, 1972, PD

In the last chapter we considered some of the events and conditions that led to Walter's decision to break bad. In this chapter we've looked at the influence of family concerns, and especially Walter's image of himself as husband and father, but none of this explains the decision to adopt the Heisenberg persona. Walter was in the RV, happily making meth several days before he decided to call himself Heisenberg.

We understand change is going to be important throughout this amazing voyage, and we saw two 180-degree changes that precipitated Walter's adoption of the Heisenberg posture.

The first course reversal was dramatically portrayed in the introduction to Episode 1.06. Walter's verbal pledge of "No more bloodshed, no violence" was juxtaposed with flash-forward visuals of a bloodied and angry Walter leaving Tuco's bunker, money bag in hand, walking past the burning, smoking, shattered fragments of the drug lord's bombed-out lair. Events early in the episode led Walter to abandon his pledge of violence-free drug manufacture.

The dramatic turning point occurred in the hospital room where Walter experienced first-hand the outcome of Jesse's attempted drug negotiation with Tuco.

Pain and Suffering

"Yo," Skinny Pete said, "I didn't catch your name."

Walter looked sick as he sat down in the chair next to Jesse's hospital bed, across the room from Skinny Pete. He didn't respond to Skinny's inquiry.

I think it is possible to believe that Walter wasn't prepared at that moment to offer his real name or an alias. More likely, I think, is the possibility that Walter was psychologically overcome and unable to process anything in his mind beyond the nearly fatal pummeling Jesse had received at the hands of Tuco.

Walter glanced one final time at Jesse. He seemed more nauseated than angry. Contextually, we are to understand Walter's feelings were not induced by the cancer treatments, but by Jesse's critical condition. "Tell me about this Tuco," Walter told Skinny Pete. "Tell me everything about him."

The next morning, Junior greeted "Bad-ass dad," who arrived at the breakfast table sporting a freshly-shaved head. Skyler's response was discomfort, to the point of almost crying. What Skyler saw as a sign of her husband's frailty and mortality, her son preferred to interpret as evidence of strength and depth of character.

Later in the day, when Walter confronted Tuco, he wore only the jacket and the shaved head, no dark glasses or pork pie hat.

"What's your name," Tuco asked.

"Heisenberg."

Walter didn't need the hat, but several other critical elements were required. The cancer, of course, which forced the bald head. But the projection of a persona was far more important, as we learned at breakfast earlier that day. Walter's baldness had to be understood as an outward sign of his inner resolve and extraordinary strength. Mercury fulminate was the crown that placed Heisenberg above Tuco in the "bad-ass" category. It was the proof that Heisenberg could be crazier and more deadly than even the unpredictable and dangerous Tuco Salamanca, but that was not the character trait that propelled him to a position of superiority over Tuco. Drug lords get into pissing matches on a regular basis, but in the end it is not guns that win wars, it is charisma. Wars are won by the sustained commitment of soldiers willing to risk their lives. Soldiers will commit to the highest order of risk only if their leader is someone they can believe in, a person they can trust to overcome the enemy.

The mercury fulminate was important, then, not so much because of its lethal force—its ability to pop eardrums and blow out windows—but because it was the crystalline icon in a grand deception successfully leveled against Tuco. Heisenberg could play meaner and tougher than anyone else in the game, but he was to be feared because he could outsmart everyone else. Tuco was unpredictable but stupid. Heisenberg was unpredictable but crafty, imaginative, eerily intelligent. His piercing eyes spoke of a mental resourcefulness that outstripped the petty bounds of "street smarts."

Piled on top of all this was crystal-pure audacity.

Tuco: "It's your meeting. Why don't you start talking and tell me what you want.
Walter: Fifty thousand dollars.
Tuco: [Laughing] Oh, man … [Laughing] Fifty Gs! How you figure that?
Walter: Thirty five for the pound of meth you stole, and another fifteen for my partner's pain and suffering.

He could have demanded anything. Fifteen thousand dollars for finding a new partner who wasn't beaten up and essentially useless, for instance. Fifteen thousand dollars so Walter could set up his own business without Jesse.

The question I asked myself during this episode began with the introduction. "The chemistry is my realm," Walter told Jesse. "Out there on the street, you deal with that." Jesse's responsibility was the selling side of the business, the part of the operation presumably beyond Walter's skill level. "This operation is you and me." For five episodes we were led to understand that Walter's inexperience in the drug trade would prevent him from interacting in a competent manner with distributors and kingpins. Walter **needed** Jesse because of the two of them only Jesse knew how to sell. This division of expertise was the single fact responsible for their unlikely partnership.

Episode 1.06 changed all the partnership parameters and forced us to scramble for a new understanding of Jesse's relationship with Walter. Heisenberg's commanding performance demonstrated in convincing manner that he possessed both the gumption and ability to deal with the most difficult and unstable personalities in the business. In fact, where Jesse had failed, Heisenberg succeeded.

Walter didn't need Jesse.

The Real Heisenberg

I believe the nature of the relationship between Walter and Jesse is the sublime question posed at the end of Season One. We know Jesse is an equal member in the partnership. But if he no longer offers business acumen that Walter lacks, what is his value to the partnership? This is not a rhetorical question. I do not argue here that Jesse really had no value, that his value has evaporated, that he is now expendable. Any such conclusion or inference would be incorrect and would not address the reality of the philosophical difficulty posed by the last one and a quarter episodes of the first season. Even stripped of his business contribution, Jesse is critical to the partnership.

It seems to me obvious that Jesse's profound value is found not in the realm of business, but in personal areas. Something about Jesse is necessary to Walter/Heisenberg's psychological or emotional wellbeing. But that statement does not even begin to address the question. The crux of the problem is that we now have two characters whose needs must be understood: Walter and Heisenberg. This is not rhetorical, either. The extent to which Heisenberg is real and differs in substantive ways from Walter White I believe to be critical to the complete understanding of Breaking Bad.

Is Heisenberg only a blustering façade that has no real connection to anyone or anything, other than to serve as vehicle for Walter's desires? Or is there a depth to Walter's creation that may eclipse the surrendering, incompetent, impotent, emasculated Walter White?

In *The Strange Case of Dr. Jekyll and Mr. Hyde*, Dr. Jekyll's body became inhabited by two diametrically opposed personalities: the original Dr. Jekyll and the diabolical, lusting, murderous Mr. Hyde. Mr. Hyde eventually asserted such control that by the end of the novella Dr. Jekyll was forced to resign. Dr. Jekyll wrote:

Will Hyde die upon the scaffold? or will he find courage to release himself at the last moment? God knows; I am careless; this is my true hour of death, and what is to follow concerns another than myself. Here then, as I lay down the pen and proceed to seal up my confession, I bring the life of that unhappy Henry Jekyll to an end.

Will Heisenberg, likewise, crowd out Walter and claim everything that was once Walter's as his own? Or will Heisenberg come out only at Walter's beck and call? Will Heisenberg become more real than Walter, or will he remain nothing more than a posture for business, a feared but fictional persona in the drug world?

As I stated above, the decision to break bad was not connected to the choice to become Heisenberg. I believe Walter became Heisenberg at a specific moment in Episode Six. It was not in his confrontation with Tuco. By then he had already chosen his persona. It was not before he entered Jesse's hospital room.

"Yo, I didn't catch your name."

It was when Walter sat down next to Jesse, feeling Jesse's pain, becoming nauseated by the young man's suffering, that Walter formulated his silent response to Skinny Pete's question. "My name is Heisenberg," he told himself.

Walter became Heisenberg in direct response to Jesse's pain.

Walter White could use science to overcome his empathy for Krazy 8; Heisenberg had no such ability, since Heisenberg was guided not by science, but by desire. Walter White, materialistic scientist, could live life in a psychological bubble, disconnected from family and friends, estranged from wife and son. Heisenberg, desire-driven drug mastermind, enjoyed no capacity for emotional withdrawal. He had to achieve human intimacy, as we saw in the opening scenes of Episode 1.07. Skyler was not making love with Walter in the Aztek outside the high school building; Heisenberg was raping her.

Skyler: Where did that come from? Why was it so good?
Walter: Because it was illegal.

It was illegal because it was not Walter, it was Heisenberg. If you doubt that Heisenberg was the one in the car, if you doubt that he was raping Skyler, hold your doubts until Season Two, Episode One, Scene Five, and we will discuss the question again.

Heisenberg could force sexual intimacy on Skyler a few times perhaps before she realized she was not being groped and compromised and penetrated by Walter, but by some other man. But he could achieve only distant connection with anyone else. For instance, he could dance around the question of the illicit pleasure of Hank's Cuban cigars, but he could never come out and say, "I make the best meth in all of New Mexico. I can't tell you what a pleasure it is to be the absolute best at something." He could never have intimacy or even true friendship with Hank.

Most painful to Walter, though, must have been the fact that he could never have real father-son intimacy with Walter Junior. This must have caused greater anguish than any kind of emotional estrangement from Skyler.

Junior, after all, exhibited all the signs of having real love for his father, and confidence in his masculinity. "Bad-ass dad" was a compliment, an assertion that his father was strong. Skyler, on the other hand, had to express nonverbal alarm at Walter's frail appearance, with his newly shaved head, because in her mind Walter had always been feeble, emasculated, not a true husband.

But Walter could never bring Junior into the meth lab. "I make the purest methamphetamine in all of the Southwestern United States. Aren't you proud of me, son?" Junior could never be proud of such an accomplishment, and therefore Walter could never share with his own son the greatest single achievement of his life—the singular proof of the value and virtue contained in the pride he felt for himself.

Jesse, on the other hand, was already a protégé, already demanding of his work the same high quality he saw in Walter's careful technique and scientific artistry.

Heisenberg is more a family man than Walter White. Walter could shrug his shoulders and leave his wife and son. Heisenberg, on the other hand, desperately needed Skyler and Junior. He could force himself on Skyler—at least in Episode 1.06. But he could not force himself to be any more of a father to Junior, could not allow Junior into emotional intimacy, because that close sphere was illegal, toxic to a teenage boy, antithetical to the father-son relationship.

With no way to achieve a close father-son bond with Junior, Heisenberg looked around for other sources of intimacy. And there he sat, in a hospital room, a few floor tiles away from a young man not five years older than his biological son.

"I am Heisenberg" is synonymous with the statement never uttered in Season One, but built into the foundation of the edifice we know as Breaking Bad: "I am Jesse's father."

Epilogue

What is the sound of one hand clapping?

As you have gathered from the tone of this book, I consider that any of us trying to make sense of Breaking Bad are participants in the drama, not merely viewers or observers. In fact, my strong bias is to believe that no one attempting legitimate understanding of noteworthy drama can simply sit back and allow the story to wash over her. She must be involved, she must participate.

"Crossed Book and Quill"
United States Navy, 2011, PD

In the same way, writing is not an exercise I conduct in a vacuum. As readers of this book, you are participants no less than me, the publisher, Martin Woutisseth, Michael Rainey, or anyone else connected with this work. In fact, your participation in this book is more important than mine. I speak here not of any academic theory of communication, but of very practical matters related to the give-and-take that brings form and substance to the world of writing and publishing. *You* are vital to that enterprise.

This book is independently written and published. I do not work for any writing house or publisher. While this affords me a tremendous degree of freedom in the types of books I can offer you, it also means that my books are not backed by any advertising department.

As you may have guessed, *you* are the advertising department for this book, and for any books I have written. Fortunately, though, you are not obliged to work eight hours a day as part of your participation in this book. In fact, if you commit to nothing more than *four or five minutes of your time*, you *can have an extraordinary impact on this book* and its ability to reach other interested reader-participants.

If you found this book entertaining, useful, or helpful in your enjoyment or understanding of Breaking Bad, I would be grateful if you could visit the online retailer where you purchased this book. Go to that retailer's page for this book, *Breaking White*, and leave a brief review of this book.

Honest reviews by customers have a greater impact on sales (and therefore book availability) than any other form of advertising, including celebrity endorsements. I would rather receive your honest review than the endorsement of any actor or celebrity associated with Breaking Bad, because your review is far more helpful.

Use any criteria you wish to attach a point value (or number of stars or whatever system is used at the retailer). If you wish me to write more books of this type in the future, a 4- or 5-star rating will be most helpful to achieving your goal. But I will be grateful for any honest review.

Reviews are precious to me, and to every independent writer. Your review counts, and counts a lot. I typically sell over 1200 copies of a book before receiving a single review. That means very slow sales, but more importantly, it means that people who might otherwise have enjoyed the book will never get to read it. So, do your part! Help others enjoy this book, and voice your opinion regarding the value of my contribution to our Breaking Bad dialog: Leave an honest review of this book.

Thank you so much for considering this request. I will see you next season in the RV!

PM
October 15, 2012

Participant Notes

Participant Notes

<u>Participant Notes</u>

Made in the USA
Lexington, KY
09 March 2014